CHINESE HIGHER EDUCATION

CHINESE HIGHER EDUCATION

A Decade of Reform and Development (1978-1988)

Ruiqing Du

Associate Professor
Xi' an Foreign Language University

St. Martin's Press
New York

To my wife and daughter

© Ruiqing Du 1992

First published in the United States of America in 1992

ISBN 0-312-06071-8

Library of Congress Cataloging-in-Publication Data

Du, Ruiqing.
    Chinese higher education : a decade of reform and development /
Ruiqing Du.
        p.   cm.
    Includes bibliographical references (p.   ) and index.
    ISBN 0-312-06071-8
    1. Eduction, Higher—China—History—20th Century. 2. Higher
education and state—China—History—20th century. 3. Educational
change—China—History—20th century.   I. Title.
    LA1133.D8   1992
    378.51—dc20

                                                    91-24251
                                                        CIP

CONTENTS

LIST OF TABLES

DEFINITIONS OF TERMS

1. Reform: Modification and/or abandonment of undesirable ways of doing things, by adopting policy decisions from higher authorities or initiating bottom-up changes, in the interest of improving the institution or the system of institutions.
2. Development: Changes in institutional policies and procedures resulting from the implementation of reform measures.
3. "Four Modernizations": Goals for the present Chinese economic development originally put forward by Zhou Enlai in 1975, namely: modernization of agriculture, industry, national defense and science and technology.
4. "Four Cardinal Principles": Principles first stated by Deng Xiaoping in a 1979 speech and later adopted by the CCP as guidelines for China's modernization. These principles are: the socialist road, the people's democratic dictatorship, the leadership of the Communist Party of China and Marxism-Leninism-Mao Zedong thought.
5. Higher education with Chinese characteristics: A distinctly Chinese-style higher education system combining its own tradition with patterns and practices adapted from the systems of other, especially industrialized, countries.
6. "Iron Rice Bowl": Common and popular term for a secure government job. Coined in the early 1980s during China's economic reform, the term refers to a system characterized by a lack of personal responsibility with regard to specific rules which tie performance to assignment, reward, punishment, dismissal and retirement of employees.
7. State: The term is used in the book to refer to the Chinese government at the central level.
8. College: Generic term for institutions of higher learning.

PREFACE

While this account of higher education in China during the decade 1978-1988 was reported using essentially historical method, it is interlaced liberally with my personal interpretations and views. This was done for three reasons: 1) I lived through this period personally and in the midst of the reforms and developments as a primary source in the roles of a faculty member and administrator in higher education; 2) the brevity and recency of the period allowed for some deviation from pure historical approaches and 3) little material of true historical perspective was available.

I am deeply indebted to the faculty members of the Department of Educational Leadership of Brigham Young University in the United States, and particularly to Dr. Curtiss Hungerford, for their constant encouragement and guidance while I was preparing the manuscript. I would also like to express my deep appreciation to educational leaders, colleagues and friends in China for providing me with valuable information and statistics. In addition, I must extend my special gratitude to Xi'an Foreign Language University headed by Professor Sun Tianyi for granting me the leave of absence to pursue Ph.D. studies in educational leadership at Brigham Young University. Without this opportunity, the present book would not have been conceived and written. Finally, I would like to give sincere thanks to my wife and daughter for their understanding, patience and love. To them this book is dedicated.

Ruiqing Du

A LIST OF ABBREVIATIONS

1. CAS: Chinese Academy of Sciences
2. CASS: Chinese Academy of Social Sciences
3. CCP: The Chinese Communist Party
4. CCPUC: the university committee of the CCP
5. CEAIE: Chinese Education Association for International Exchange
6. CEN: *China Exchange News*
7. CIER: Central Institute for Educational Research
8. IIE: Institute of International Education
9. KMT: Kuomintang, the Nationalist Party
10. PLA: The People's Liberation Army
11. PRC: The People's Republic of China
12. SEC: The State Education Commission under the State Council of the People's Republic of China
13. UNESCO: The United Nations Education, Science and Culture Organization

INTRODUCTION

"**E**ducation should be geared toward modernization, the world, and the future." This guideline by Deng Xiaoping (1983), chief architect of the Chinese reform in the 1980s, charted a new course for the development of Chinese education. Instead of serving "proletarian politics" (CCP, 1958), as was the case before 1978, Chinese education began to serve primarily "socialist construction" (CCP, 1985), to interact with foreign countries and to contribute significantly to the building of China into a modern, powerful nation "before the end of the century" (CCP, 1978).

To build the relatively poor and backward China into a modern, powerful nation within some 20 years presented a particularly great challenge to institutions of higher learning which are "charged with the important task of training advanced specialized personnel" (CCP, 1985) urgently needed for this ambitious goal. Therefore, with the shift in emphasis, a series of policy readjustments had been made in Chinese higher education with regard to management, structure, curriculum, students, faculty and exchanges with other countries. These reform measures brought about major changes in Chinese higher education. The number of institutions of higher learning doubled from 598 in 1978 to 1075 in 1988. Enrollment reached 2.1 million in 1988, 2.4 times the 1978 figure (*Guangming Daily*, September, 22, 1989, p. 2). Besides the growth in numbers and enrollments, Chinese higher education experienced a dramatic diversification of institutional types and echelons: two- or three-year colleges devoted to vocational and technical programs had been established; private colleges and universities, which had been closed after the Communists came to power in 1949, reappeared; adult education institutions mushroomed (SEC, 1988, p. 28). In addition, the former rigid and excessive governmental control had gradually been replaced by a relatively flexible management system under the guidance of unified educational policies and plans of the state (CCP, 1985). By 1988 the reform of Chinese higher education was still continuing with much vigor. Building on its own strengths and absorbing salient features of foreign patterns and practices, a new Chinese higher education system was slowly but steadily taking shape.

All these achievements were made against the background of a complex and dynamic political context. The nation's shift of emphasis from class struggle to economic development and the subsequent adoption of an open-door policy since 1978 marked a turning point in the history of China (Hayhoe, 1989, p. 3). The repudiation of the ravages and havoc wrought by the "Gang of Four" during the Cultural Revolution (1966-76) and, accompanying it, the "elimination of chaos and restoration of order" (CCP, 1985) throughout the country paved the way for full-scale economic development, which, in turn, called for and promoted extensive social, political and educational reforms aimed at modernizing China's agriculture, industry, national defense and science and technology. To modernize the country, it was essential for China to learn from the advanced science and technology and managerial skills and to obtain financial assistance from the United States and other industrialized countries. Therefore, China modified its foreign policies and started reaching out to the West. Realizing China as a huge potential market and a major political power in global diplomacy, the United States and other industrialized nations quickly responded to Chinese initiatives. The subsequent diplomatic ties, trade and technological cooperation and cultural and educational exchanges which had been negotiated and established in quick succession not only began to revitalize the Chinese economy, but also gave impetus to the reform and development of Chinese higher education.

The reform and development of Chinese higher education during the important decade (1978-1988) attracted the attention of scholars in many parts of the world (Hayhoe, 1989; Orleans, 1988; Qu, 1988; Hao and Wang, 1987; Huang, 1987, 1985; Cleverley, 1985; Gu, 1984; Henze, 1984; Pepper, 1982; Gardner, 1982). But critical and analytic studies seemed to be sparse and sporadic. Very little research dealing with the dynamics and complexities of the whole spectrum of the reform and development had been published. A current, comprehensive study was, therefore, needed to review and report the major efforts of the reform and development of Chinese higher education during the decade. It is hoped that the findings of this study would be useful in planning for the immediate and the long-range future of Chinese higher education and in promoting the understanding of contemporary Chinese higher education by scholars in the rest of the world.

In examining the reform and development of Chinese higher education during the decade 1978 to 1988, answers to the following questions were sought:

1) What were the highlights of Chinese higher education prior to 1978 that provided perspectives for the decade 1978 to 1988?

2) What reform measures were initiated in the management and structure of Chinese higher education?
3) What reform measures were initiated in the curriculum and instruction of Chinese higher education?
4) What reform measures were initiated in student recruitment and placement?
5) What measures were undertaken for faculty development?
6) What kinds of exchange programs with other countries were developed and what problems emerged as a result?

After the discussion of these questions, the book analyzed China's specific conditions in relation to its education and attempted to predict the development of Chinese higher education into the last decade of the twentieth century and beyond.

The research into such an historic period of Chinese higher education had to be based on the availability of data, both primary and secondary sources. The primary sources of data for this research consisted of the following:

1) policy decisions covering different aspects of Chinese higher education formulated and promulgated by Chinese authorities. These documents were available in Chinese or in English translations.
2) reports of innovations and experiments published in an increasing number of journals on higher education by educational administrative organizations and individual institutions in China.
3) interviews or correspondence with Chinese students, scholars and educational leaders.

The bulk of the statistical information for this study came from documents, newspaper reports, journal articles and speeches by Chinese Party and government leaders. Other sources of the statistical data were taken from the reports by the World Bank and UNESCO in their study of China in close collaboration with the Chinese government.

The secondary sources of data for this study were drawn from the research by scholars in many parts of the world. Though not large in number, these books or articles dealing with specific problems of Chinese higher education contained solid research, in-depth analyses and thought-provoking insights. But to avoid an excess of secondary information, which may pose "a major problem with much historical research" (Gay, 1987, p. 10), the use of these data was kept to a minimum.

Higher education in China consists of two distinct sectors: full-time traditional institutions of higher learning and full-time/part-time/spare-time nontraditional institutions of higher learning. This book concentrated only on the traditional sector of higher education unless otherwise specifically noted and discussed.

1

Chinese Higher Education: An Historical Overview

Higher education in China has been molded and influenced by a variety of forces. On the one hand there was the pervasive feudal thinking, represented by the doctrines of Confucius, dominating every facet of Chinese higher education until recent times. On the other hand there were, in the modern period, persistent foreign patterns either infiltrated into the country following the aggression by foreign powers or modeled consciously by the Chinese out of political and economic considerations. These influences, Confucian and foreign, were further compounded by frequent policy swings of the CCP in the 1950s and 1960s in an attempt to shape higher education for political reasons. It was only during the last decade (1978-88) that relatively systematic and balanced efforts began to be made to develop higher education in light of China's socioeconomic conditions and by critical assimilation of foreign practices. Therefore, the history of Chinese higher education has been a process of constant change since ancient times.

Ancient Times (Sixteenth Century B.C. to 1840)

Chinese higher education dates back in its embryonic forms to the later period of the Shang Dynasty (1523-1027 B.C.) when the foundations of Chinese culture—music, art, written language, literature, the calendar, astronomy, medicine and history—had already been laid (Cai, 1982, p. 9 and Gu, 1984). At the time schools were run by the government to train officials. The teachers were government officials. The main subjects taught were the Six Arts, namely: Rites (rituals and rules), Music, Archery, Chariot-Riding,

History and Mathematics (CHEC, 1983, p. 1). With the disintegration of the slave system, these government-run schools fell into disarray and began to be replaced by private institutions of higher learning during the Spring-Autumn and Warring States periods (770-221 B.C.).

Confucius (551-479 B.C.), the leading thinker and educator of the time, played a key role in advancing ancient Chinese education. He held that human nature was good and, therefore, the goal of education was to cultivate and develop human nature so that virtue and wisdom and ultimately moral perfection would be attained. Once reaching moral perfection, a man would be in harmony with his fellow human beings and become capable of regulating worldly affairs (1966).

Based on this theory, Confucius and his disciples advocated that education should be made available to all regardless of social class. Moreover, anyone who studied diligently and competed successfully through examinations should be made an official. In fact, Confucius selected his students from all strata of society. Upon completing their studies, the students went forth to serve as civil servants and teachers. These ideas and practices of Confucius, coupled with his pedagogical thinking, laid the foundation for feudal Chinese higher education over a period of more than 2000 years. In fact, Confucian philosophy dominated almost every aspect of Chinese life until the Communists came to power in 1949.

The curriculum of Confucius-inspired higher education was comprised of The Four Books (*The Analects of Confucius, Mencius, The Great Learning* and *The Doctrine of the Mean*) and The Five Classics (*The Book of Odes, The Book of Documents, The Book of Rites, The Book of Change* and *The Spring and Autumn Annals*). These books, which contained principles with regard to government and the administration of society as well as maxims of personal conduct, constituted the essence of Confucian thinking, which was made the state ideology in the Western Han Dynasty (202 B.C.-9 A.D.). Although courses in mathematics and astronomy and in such professional areas as medicine and pharmacology were added in the Tang Dynasty (618-907 A.D.), the peak of China's feudal society, the Confucian classics remained the predominant curricular content throughout the feudal times. Very little instruction in technical or practical subjects was emphasized. There was "a clear hierarchy of prestige with the pure knowledge of classical principles of socio-political order holding absolute sway over such richly developed techniques as engineering, medicine, mathematics and chemistry" (Hayhoe, 1989, p. 13). But in spite of the predominance of Confucian classics both in curriculum and prestige, unorthodox texts such as those of Daoism and Buddhism were adopted in later dynasties. And in the private academies during the Song, Yuan, Ming and Qing Dynasties (960 to 1911 A.D.), free discussions and debates, which could be very critical of the ruling classes, directed self-study and research also became common practice (Cai, pp. 33-35).

The Confucian idea of educational equality provided the rationale for the imperial examination system administered by the government and aimed at selecting and recruiting officials on the basis of individual merit. The examinations were exacting and rigid, requiring the candidates to memorize vast amounts of material in classics and to write essays in a fixed style.

The selection and recruitment of able officials did not, however, mean government support for education during the successive feudal dynasties. Although the examinations and the resultant academic degrees and ascendancy to power were the dream of many aspiring young and often middle-aged scholars, few could afford the expenses for attending high-quality private academies and receiving a solid education which would enable them to pass the challenging examinations at various levels. It followed that education, though highly valued and eagerly sought, was difficult to achieve and remained accessible only to a minority of people made up mostly of wealthy, powerful landowners and aristocrats.

Modern Period (1840-1949)

The defects of China's feudal higher education system were manifestly exposed after China's defeat in the Opium War (1840-1842) and the ensuing subjection to a semicolonial status by invading Western powers (Fairbank and Reischauer, 1978, p. 277). What followed then was a series of reforms championed by a group of bourgeois reformists. As a result, science and technology courses were officially added to the curriculum, which was up till then comprised largely of Confucian classics in the existing institutions. In addition, new types of schools were established: foreign-language training institutions, technical colleges and military academies. "By 1895, there were in existence 22 establishments dedicated exclusively to the specific branches of Western knowledge" (Bastid, 1987). Meanwhile, overseas studies of advanced Western science and technology began. By 1875, the Chinese government had sent 125 students to the United States (Cai, p. 125). Later, after the Sino-Japanese War of 1894, hundreds of students went to Japan (Fairbank and Reischauer, pp. 39-40).

Reforms toward the late nineteenth century were aimed at building up the country through education and saving China from falling prey to aggression and subjugation by foreign powers. The express principle was to promote Chinese learning (mainly Confucian classics) as the core or essence and to include Western knowledge for utilization (Cai, p. 127, and Bastid, 1987). Though much had been achieved in the reform movement, the foundation of the feudal system remained basically untouched. Loyalty to the emperor and filial piety to one's forefathers were still strictly enforced. All the students studying overseas were subjected to close surveillance by government-sent officials. Any disloyalty to the emperor and the feudal regime would result in immediate repatriation and severe punishment (Cai, p. 126).

But the bourgeois revolution in 1911 in the wake of the late nineteenth-century reforms brought about more radical changes in China's burgeoning modern higher education system. With the impact of the revolution, the Qing Dynasty academies were converted to public institutions, the imperial examinations and all the required courses on Confucian classics were abolished, and the vernacular began to be used in teaching and textbooks in place of the classical language. In their attempt to build a modern higher education system, the bourgeois democrats had to choose and decide which model to follow, which foreign system had an approach to knowledge that was best suited to China, which was at the time a semifeudal and semicolonial country in the throes of civil war and economic collapse. In a way, the presence of the schools run by foreign missionary organizations and, above all, the foreign domination of China forced the Chinese educated elites to make such a choice.

At the time, European, American and Japanese influences on Chinese higher education were discernible either through the institutions these countries had set up in China or through the management of education by returned Chinese scholars who had studied in these countries. But cultural similarity, geographical proximity, identical need for national self-strengthening and a large contingent of Japanese-trained scholars made it natural for the Chinese to follow the Japanese model in the beginning. However, when China was plunged into chaos following the breakdown of the central authority and the fighting among warlords during the early 1920s, the American educational system, with its democratic and progressive ideas and less rigid and authoritarian management pattern, proved to be more congenial to China than those of Europe and Japan. A movement for educational reforms initiated and led primarily by scholars returned from the United States, many of whom had been former students of John Dewey at Columbia University, resulted in a higher education system in China very similar to American patterns. The curriculum was organized within colleges, which consisted of departments. A general first year preceded the choosing of specialized courses of study, and the credit system was adopted to make sure that the student embraced a broad range of knowledge (Hayhoe, p. 26, and Wang, 1936).

This predominance of American influence, however, did not exclude the adoption and adaptation of the elements of other foreign systems. In fact, the Chinese borrowed selectively from a number of sources—English, German, French, Japanese as well as American—in their efforts to modernize the Chinese higher education system (Hayhoe, p. 82, and Bastid). Furthermore, though China had fallen victim in the early twentieth century to imperialist powers with foreign domination of its political sovereignty and plunder of its economic resources, education remained largely the prerogative of the Chinese government (Bastid). By a series of legislative measures in the late 1920s and early 1930s, the national government defined and enforced unified entrance requirements, graduation examinations and a curricular structure for all universities and independent colleges. Private colleges and universities were also required by law to conform to the national scheme. The campuses of the 30 institutions of higher learning of American origin which "reflected American curriculum, architecture, and methods of education" gradually took on "more Chinese flavor and more cosmopolitan characteristics" (Barrow, 1948).

So the modernization of Chinese higher education began largely as a forced response to foreign invasion, but Chinese higher education did not experience an intellectual dependency. The borrowing and integration of foreign elements of higher education had a liberating effect on Chinese higher education rather than subordinating it to any one system. There was no denying that civil war and foreign aggression impeded the development of a viable and effective higher education system, but given the circumstances at the time, achievements were significant. Whether government supported or privately operated, there existed in China a sizable number of colleges and universities offering a wide range of disciplines and technical specialties before the founding of the PRC in 1949 (see Table 1.1). Some universities and specialized colleges were, in fact, outstanding (Croizier, 1979). Side by side with these public, private and missionary colleges and universities in the Kuomingtang (KMT) controlled regions during the first half of the century, a new type of higher education emerged in the areas held by the CCP to meet the need of the Communist revolution and the War of Resistance Against Japan. This kind of education was developed "in conscious reaction to Western education systems which had been imposed on China for some decades with uneven success" (Hayhoe, 1984). These new institutions established by the CCP and kept in operation during the 14 years from 1936 to 1949 fell into the following categories: cadre-training for

Table 1.1

Type and Number of Chinese Institutions of Higher Learning in 1949

TYPE	NUMBER
Comprehensive universities	49
Engineering	28
Agriculture	18
Medicine & pharmacology	22
Teacher training	12
Language and literature	11
Finance & economics	11
Political science & law	7
Physical culture	2
Arts	18
Other	27
TOTAL	**205**

Source: Ministry of Education (MOE), 1985. *Achievement of Education in China.* Beijing: People's Education Press, p. 50.

military affairs and civil administrative duties, arts, sciences, medicine, agriculture, commerce and engineering. Though ill-equipped, irregular in length of study and restricted in course offerings, they trained a large contingent of officials and technical personnel for practical purposes and became models for the educational development throughout the late 1950s and during the years of the Cultural Revolution (1966-1976). After 1949 when the CCP took control of the whole country and moved into cities, these institutions were either discontinued or incorporated into other traditional universities. A few of these institutions served as the basis for a number of newly established colleges and universities patterned on the Soviet model.

Contemporary Period (1949 to Present)

The Founding of the PRC to the Cultural Revolution (1949-1966)

The founding of the People's Republic of China marked a great turning point for Chinese higher education. It put an end to the civil war and the colonization of China by imperialist powers and ushered in a period of political stability, rapid economic growth and cultural and educational development. In accordance with its Marxist-Leninist ideology, the Communist government repudiated and rejected the semifeudal and semicolonial system of higher education and, step by step, gained complete control of all the colleges and universities left over by the KMT government or supported by foreign missionary organizations. Measures were taken to build up a new higher education system within a social milieu of conformity to the line and policies of the CCP.

First, an extensive restructuring of the existing institutions of higher learning began. By a series of centrally mandated administrative measures, comprehensive universities consisting of liberal arts, science, engineering, agriculture, political science, law and medicine were eliminated. Former colleges of engineering, medicine and agriculture within comprehensive universities were split off or combined with similar departments of former independent colleges or transformed into specialized colleges or technical institutes. Four major types of institutions of higher learning emerged as a result of the reorganization: 1) comprehensive universities with liberal arts and sciences; 2) polytechnical colleges and universities with a wide range of applied scientific fields; 3) independent colleges with specialties in engineering, agriculture, medicine, business administration, political science, law, languages and literature, arts and physical culture and 4) institutions for the training of teachers. By the end of 1953 when the restructuring had been basically completed, the universities were reduced to 14, while the number of specialized colleges showed a marked increase (see Table 1.2). With the restructuring, the former three-level university-college-department administrative hierarchy was replaced by a two-level university-department structure. The department was given a clear disciplinary identity and was further divided by narrow specializations. Students were recruited into a given specialization with a fixed time requirement instead of a credit-hour system.

Equally important as the restructuring, Chinese higher education came under the control of the centrally planned economic development. Centralized entrance examinations for the college-bound, unified job assignments for the graduates, stipends and free tuition for undergraduate and graduate students and fixed pay scales for faculty members were instituted by central government decrees. Administratively, the comprehensive and polytechnical universities and teacher-training institutions were placed under the control of the national Ministry of Higher Education (MOE). Special colleges were mostly placed under the authority of other related ministries under the central government. The curriculum for each specialization was designed and developed at the national level by committees made up of professors from

Table 1.2

**Type and Number of Chinese Institutions of Higher Learning
in 1947 and 1953**

TYPE	NUMBER	
	1947 *	1953
Comprehensive university	55	14
Engineering	18	38
Agriculture	18	26
Forestry	—	3
Medicine & pharmacology	23	29
Teacher training	22	33
Language & literature	4	8
Finance & economics	10	6
Political science & law	—	4
Physical culture	5	4
Arts	15	15
Other	37	1
TOTAL	**207**	**181**

* 1947 is considered the peak year of higher education development before 1949.

Source: Ministry of Education (MOE), 1985. *Achievement of Education in China.*
Beijing: People's Education Press, pp. 50, 51.

prestigious institutions chosen and guided by the Ministry of Higher Education. Courses in Communist theory replaced the Confucian classics as compulsory subjects. In line with the socialist principle of providing comprehensive care for every employee, all institutions of higher learning were made residential, as was every other social establishment. Houses or apartments were allocated to faculty and staff at nominal rent, and lodging was provided for students free of charge.

Having rejected the patterns of the industrialized powers and the Nationalist government by means of restructuring and administrative change and finding their educational experience during the war years inadequate for the comprehensive economic development, the Chinese Communists looked to the Soviet Union for a possible model to emulate in the formative years of the People's Republic. This was not only necessary but also feasible in the political context—the Chinese had learned Marxism from the Soviets, the two ruling parties pursued the same goals, and the two nations shared the same social systems. With brotherly Sino-Soviet relations and Russian influence dominating China's economic, military and scientific realms, it was inevitable that Chinese higher education would bear a strong Russian imprint.

Apart from the nationwide, Soviet-inspired reorganization of institutional types, there followed also a successive adoption of Russian teaching plans, course outlines, textbooks and instructional methods. Russian advisors and professors were employed to guide the development of China's higher education or to engage in exemplary teaching and research. From 1952 to 1956, Russian textbooks translated and published in China and used as classroom texts or major reference materials numbered 1393 titles. By the end of 1957, 63 Chinese universities and colleges had established exchange relations with their Soviet and East European counterparts. From 1949 to 1960 when the two parties broke off relations, 861 Russians served as advisors, professors or researchers in Chinese educational administrative organs and institutions of higher learning. As many as 8424 Chinese students and scholars were sent to the Soviet Union and 1109 to its satellite countries to study or receive technical training. For over a decade, Russian took the place of English as the predominant foreign language, which was a compulsory course for Chinese university students. In addition, classroom procedures, the organization of the subject matter, the five-point grading system and the collective effort of teachers in preparing their lessons were all duplicated from the Soviet model (Huang, 1987). This indiscriminate transplanting of the Soviet pattern in the early and mid-1950s had a striking parallel with the attempts of bourgeois reformists and democrats to introduce Western and Japanese practices in the late nineteenth and early twentieth centuries. The emulation of Western and Japanese systems had been liberating in effect, marking a break with feudal tradition and the creation of a progressive and modern one. The wholesale and uncritical borrowing from the Soviet Union, however, pushed Chinese higher education toward centralization and authoritarianism in tune with the political climate of the newly founded regime. Admittedly, large numbers of specialized and technical personnel were trained for the nation's rehabilitation and economic revitalization, but it was only a short-term gain. In the long run, the development of an effective higher education system capable of meeting the challenge of changing socioeconomic needs was hampered. The separation of science from engineering, the narrow specialization and the centralized administrative pattern began to take their toll when China embarked on the road toward broad-scale modernization in the late 1970s and early 1980s.

Fortunately, the Chinese became aware, from the late 1950s on, of the potential harm this wholesale borrowing might inflict on the development of higher education in China. This awareness was heightened when the ideological differences between the two ruling parties became evident and serious. The Great Leap Forward launched during 1958-1959 immediately after the height of the Sino-Soviet relationship signified a reaction to and rejection of the Soviet model and an attempt by the Chinese to establish a higher education system distinctly their own. By this time, the Chinese had determined to put an end to the mechanical and blind copying of the Soviet experience, the bulk of which was ill-suited to China. At the time, the rejection was not only necessary but also possible after the successful completion of the First Five-Year Plan (1953-1957) which had secured for China impressive economic growth.

Having broken away from the Soviet model after the nation's Five-Year Plan for economic development, the CCP formulated new educational guidelines on the basis of its experience in the 1930s and 1940s: Education must serve proletarian politics and be combined with productive labor (CCP, 1958). Consequently, the administrative power of the institutions of higher learning was taken from the professionals and put into the hands of the CCP university committee (Wu, 1988), and a much larger proportion of the student's time was spent on practical work in factories and the countryside and on social and political activities. In addition, China's Great Leap Forward, a rash attempt to expedite the nation's social and economic development in the wake of the First Five-Year Plan, brought about other changes in higher education. A variety of forms of instruction was implemented: part-time schools, evening classes and vocational training courses. Students from among high school graduates as well as people from all walks of life were enrolled in the markedly increased number of institutions of higher learning, swelling the number of students. The institutions of higher learning, in turn, registered a similar sharp growth in staff and faculty members (see Table 1.3).

This impetuous endeavor to advance higher education in disregard of the limited resources at the time was bound to fail. In fact it was soon frustrated by the economic slump attributed to natural disasters, the Soviet insistence on a colossal amount of debt payment and the withdrawal of all Soviet engineers working in most of China's key enterprises, all of which occurred in the following two years (1960-1961). Other factors brought about and hastened the failure as well. The widespread attack on and repudiation of intellectuals starting from the Anti-Rightist Campaign in 1957 incapacitated their service and dampened their enthusiasm. Moreover, the one-sided emphasis on education serving proletarian politics, the integration of education with productive labor and the flooding of students in the hastily estab-

Table 1.3

Increase of Institutions, Enrollment, Staff and Faculty of
Chinese Higher Education (1957 and 1960)

	NUMBER		INCREASE
	1957	1960	
Institutions	229	1,289	5.6
Enrollment	44,118	961,623	2.8
Staff	8,527	194,408	2.3
Faculty	70,018	139,142	2.0

Source: Ministry of Education (MOE), 1985. *Achievement of Education in China.*
Beijing: People's Education Press, pp. 50, 51.

lished institutions of higher learning exhausted the human and material
resources of higher education and led to a sharp decline in the quality of
instruction (Zhou, 1989). A period of retrenchment followed: a cutting down
of the swollen number of institutions and of enrollment and a sober reassess-
ment of the gains and blunders higher education had experienced since the
early 1950s. Compared with 1960, the 1963 and 1965 enrollment dropped
by 22 and 30 percent respectively (MOE, p. 54). Table 1.4 contrasts the
number of institutions in 1960 following the Great Leap Forward and in 1963
when the growth began to be checked.

With the realization of the damaging effect of this rash attempt and with
the improvement of the national economy, Chinese higher education had a
few years (1961-1965) of comparatively healthy and balanced development
after the wholesale borrowing from the Soviet Union and the heady years of
the Great Leap Forward. The pendulum swung away from the earlier policy
extremes to the rational and realistic consideration of an effective higher
education system suitable for Chinese conditions. The number of institutions
was duly reduced, as shown in Table 1.4, the presidents were given more
administrative power following the implementation of the president responsibility system under the CCPUC (Wu, 1988) and the intellectuals were
recognized as mental workers serving the proletariat (Chen, 1962). Also, a
1961 CCP document (*The Sixty Articles*) reiterated that the major tasks of an
institution of higher learning were teaching and learning. To guarantee
quality teaching and learning, excessive time devoted to productive labor
and social and political activities was reduced to appropriate proportions,
and the emphasis on entrance and course examinations was renewed. To

Table 1.4

Change in the Number and Type of Chinese Colleges and Universities in 1960 and 1963

TYPE	NUMBER	
	1960	**1963**
Comprehensive university	37	27
Engineering	472	120
Agriculture	180	44
Forestry	24	8
Medicine & pharmacology	204	85
Teacher training	227	61
Language and literature	8	6
Finance & economics	25	16
Political science & law	9	4
Physical culture	30	10
Arts	45	22
Other	28	2
TOTAL	**1,289**	**405**

Source: Ministry of Education (MOE), 1985. *Achievement of Education in China.* Beijing: People's Education Press, p. 51.

further improve teaching and learning, the existing colleges and universities were streamlined, and 68 prestigious and strategically important institutions were selected and designated in successive years as key universities and colleges which were guaranteed, by policy mandates, a better supply of students and priority appropriations from the national government for exemplary pacesetting roles. Other measures to ensure quality teaching and learning included reactivating national committees for textbook and curriculum development for all fields of study in accordance with specific Chinese conditions, introducing authoritative textbooks and reference materials published in major industrialized nations to bring teaching at Chinese institutions of higher learning up to the advanced world level and establishing, on a limited scale, scholarly and academic exchanges with industrialized countries in Europe.

With all these efforts, Chinese higher education entered a period of steady development. Colleges and universities began to be "well-run, although not very innovative in teaching methods" (Croizier, 1979). In 1965, one year

Table 1.5

Development of Chinese Higher Education:
A Comparison Between 1949 and 1965

	NUMBER		INCREASE
	1949	1965	
Institution	205	434	2.1
Undergraduate enrollment	116,504	674,436	5.9
Graduate enrollment	629	4,546	7.2
Faculty	16,059	138,116	8.6

Source: Ministry of Education (MOE), 1985. *Achievement of Education in China.*
Beijing: People's Education Press, pp. 50, 53, 113
Table 1.6 provides more information about Chinese higher education in 1965.

before the Cultural Revolution was launched, a viable and effective higher education system had gradually been taking shape. As illustrated in Table 1.5, the number of institutions, faculty and students all increased by a wide margin as compared with 1949. Furthermore, alternative higher education in the form of half-work and half-study schools, adult institutions, spare-time and correspondence courses trained 200,000 specialized personnel for different sectors of the economy (Cai, p. 160).

The Cultural Revolution (1966-1976)

Unfortunately, the few years of the relatively balanced development of Chinese higher education were soon interrupted. The Cultural Revolution, which was initiated by Mao Zedong in 1966, plunged the whole of China into turmoil affecting every facet of Chinese society. But it was education, especially higher education, that "suffered the most severe disruption and the most serious consequences" (Fingar and Reed, 1982). If the educational reform during the Great Leap Forward was a reaction to the Sovietization in the early 1950s, the revolution in education, which was a major component part of the Cultural Revolution, was directed against all foreign educational patterns and practices that had been introduced to or imposed on China and all previous educational systems indigenously Chinese except the experience of the Communist-run education during the 1930s and 1940s.

In the destruction of old systems and repudiation of foreign influences, Mao attempted to build an egalitarian system of education available to all and serving slavishly pure Communist ideals, only to experience a devastation of Chinese education unprecedented in Chinese history. At the height

Table 1.6

Chinese Higher Education in 1965: Specializations, Students, and Faculty

SPECIALIZATIONS		(%)	STUDENTS	(%)	FACULTY	(%)
Engineering	1,208	(42)	295,273	(43.8)	44,748	(32.4)
Agriculture	248	(8.7)	53,447	(7.9)	7,729	(5.6)
Forestry	49	(1.7)	9,793	(1.5)	1,307	(1.0)
Medicine & pharmacology	133	(4.6)	82,861	(12.3)	13,630	(10)
Teacher training	420	(15)	94,268	(14.0)	1,075	(0.8)
Humanities	303	(10.5)	46,038	(6.8)	28,017	(20)
Natural sciences	260	(9.0)	62,232	(9.2)	30,458	(22)
Finance & economics	91	(3.0)	18,119	(2.7)	1,863	(1.3)
Political science & law	8	(0.28)	4,144	(0.6	502	(0.4)
Physical culture	20	(0.7)	4,205	(0.6)	5,279	(4.0)
Arts	125	(4.4)	4,235	(0.5)	2,811	(2.0)
Other	——		——		697	(0.5)
TOTAL	**2,865**	**(100%)**	**674,615**	**(100%)**	**138,116**	**(100%)**

Source: Ministry of Education (MOE), 1985. *Achievement of Education in China.*
Beijing: People's Education Press, pp. 53, 54, 55. 100, 101.

of the Cultural Revolution, students (Red Guards) roamed the country disseminating Mao Zedong thought, mobilizing worker-peasant masses and later involving themselves in factional fighting— physical as well as verbal. Instead of engaging in academic studies, they took class struggle as their main course of study, denouncing bourgeois intellectuals, repudiating the capitalist-roaders in power and struggling to prevent China from changing its socialist orientation. All these youthful ideals and the misguided activism led to the suspension of enrollment (six years for the undergraduate and 12 years for the graduate) and the six-year suspension of academic and scholarly exchanges with other countries.

When most universities began to enroll students in 1972, peer recommendation on the basis of political virtue replaced unified entrance examinations; worker-peasant-soldier masses and junior or senior high school graduates who had been subjected to at least two years of reeducation in rural areas or factories became candidates in place of senior high school graduates; the length of schooling was shortened from the former four to six years to three years; and political cant, social activities, practical experience and manual labor substituted for serious academic pursuits. In short, the Cultural Revolution restructured the entire Chinese higher education system with the objective of eliminating the control of schools by "bourgeois intellectuals."

To terminate the bourgeois domination of education, the discredited central and provincial CCP educational administrative organs were dissolved and replaced by the loose groups under the purified CCP central committees and newly set up provincial revolutionary committees. At the institutional level, revolutionary committees made up of militant students, "well-re-molded" faculty, "trustworthy" former administrators, industrial workers, and army officers took the responsibility of management in all spheres of institutional life—political, academic and logistic. But a correct political orientation and active participation in class struggle constituted the overriding concern of the administrative duties.

In the termination of the bourgeois domination of schools, university professors, particularly the senior ones, bore the brunt of the onslaught of the Cultural Revolution. Denounced as bourgeois intellectuals, they were humiliated, physically abused and then made to reform themselves by doing manual labor on campus or in rural areas. When the Cultural Revolution ended, Chinese colleges and universities were left with a faculty disproportionate in age composition and incapable of quality teaching and research. As indicated in Table 1.7, the number of full professors in 1977 decreased by 25 percent as compared with 1965, associate professors by 19 percent and lecturers 6 percent. An increase in the total number was shown only in the categories of instructors and assistants, the vast majority of whom were retained from among the graduates during the Cultural Revolution years who had not gone through rigorous academic training. Many were later transferred to other jobs.

Not only was the development of faculty adversely affected, but also the fields of study, which had been fluctuating with violent policy swings of CCP, became more unbalanced. For example, the enrollment of students of finance and economics, which was 18,120 in 1965, comprising 2.7 of the total, was down to 6570 in 1976, only 1.2 percent of the total. The enrollment of students of political science and law dropped from the 1965 low of 4150 to 410 in 1976, 0.6 and 0.1 percent respectively of the total enrollment (MOE, 1985, pp. 54, 62). This imbalance posed a sharp contrast with pre-1949 days when finance and economics had 11.4 percent and political science and law 24.4 percent of the total enrollment (MOE, p. 62), an imbalance which took years of effort to correct in the 1980s.

Table 1.7

A Comparison of Faculty by Academic Rank at Chinese
Colleges and Universities (1965 and 1976)

RANK	1965	(%)	1976	(%)
Professor	3,056	(2.6)	2,288	(1.2)
Associate Professor	4,382	(3.2)	3,531	(1.9)
Lecturer	29,000	(21.1)	27,344	(14.8)
Instructor	11,611	(8.4)	41,319	(22.4)
Assistant	89,417	(64.7)	110,478	(59.7)
TOTAL	137,466		184,960	

Source: Ministry of Education (MOE), 1985. *Achievement of Education in China.*
Beijing: People's Education Press, pp. 102, 103.

Note: Assistants were recent graduates recruited as faculty members. After a one-year probation, they became instructors. Approximately five years were required for each other category to be eligible for promotion to the next higher category. Lecturers were equivalent to assistant professors in the United States.

Loss of library holdings and destruction of laboratory facilities and classroom buildings were also serious damages wrought by the Cultural Revolution. But most crucial of all, a whole generation of youth was deprived of the opportunity for a wholesome education. It was estimated that, because of the Cultural Revolution, China lost 1.5 million specialists (Gu, 1984) essential to the modernization of the country's relatively backward economy.

Summary

Chinese higher education has had a history extending over 3000 years. During the long feudal period, high-ranking government officials were trained in government or privately sponsored institutions and recruited through rigid imperial examinations. For thousands of years, Confucian classics formed the main curricular content. Very little instruction in technical and vocational subjects was offered at the high level. It was the scholar officials that ruled China and perpetuated the feudal higher educational system, which was, in turn, dominated by Confucian thinking and geared toward the training of government officials.

Modern Chinese higher education began in the late nineteenth century following the invasion of China by foreign powers. Its development was promoted by the efforts of bourgeois reformists and democrats in subsequent years and influenced by foreign patterns and practices—Japanese, German, French, British and, above all, American—through conscious modeling by returned scholars from these countries and the presence of foreign institutions on the Chinese soil. Curriculum at modern Chinese institutions of higher learning was much broadened, embracing a wider range of disciplines and technical specialties than before. Contemporary Chinese higher education departed markedly from the models before 1949. Upon coming to power, the CCP took control of all institutions of higher learning, both public and private, and began to reorganize and transform them in line with Communist ideology and the need of the country's economic development. In the process of reorganization and transformation, the Soviet system was taken as the best pattern under the political circumstances. Realizing in time the unsuitability of the Soviet pattern, the CCP switched, in the following years, to a succession of policies characterized by constant and often extreme swings. As a result, higher education in contemporary China followed a "tortuous course" of development (CCP, 1985). Most disastrous of all was the Cultural Revolution, which attempted in vain to overhaul Chinese higher education by negating and discarding almost all previous practices. The problems with contemporary Chinese education from 1949 to 1966 were summarized in the landmark 1985 document *Decision of the CCP Central Committee on the Reform of the Educational System*:

> Since the late 1950s, however, because of the failure to shift the emphasis of the Party's work to economic construction and the influence of the "Leftist" ideology of "taking class struggle as the key link", the educational cause, instead of being regarded as important, was repeatedly and at length rebuffed by "Leftist" political movement. Because of the Cultural Revolution, such "Leftist" mistakes even developed into radical actions, discrediting knowledge and eliminating education. Consequently, the cause of education was seriously harmed, the broad masses of educators were severely persecuted, the growth of the whole generation of young people was retarded and the already narrowed gap between China and other developed world countries in many areas of education again widened.

Recognizing the problems, the post-Mao leadership of the CCP set out, in the drastically changed political and economic situation, to reshape China's higher education.

2

Management and Structure

As indicated in the historical overview, Chinese higher education had been characterized by rigid government control. In the context of a highly centralized political and economic system, such control appeared to be not only inevitable but also necessary. And as evidenced by the achievement "unmatched among developing countries of the same income level" since 1949 and the "high quality" or even "international standard" (World Bank, 1986, p. 2), it could be said that the government control had facilitated rather than impeded the development of higher education in China.

The political and economic situation in China after 1978, however, began to change. Instead of mobilizing the masses for continual political campaigns with class struggle as the key link, the CCP switched to extensive economic revitalization. This shift in emphasis was clearly articulated at the 3rd Plenary Session of the 11th Central Committee of the CCP in 1978 and reiterated at later congresses and sessions. The objectives set for the economic development under the umbrella term of the Four Modernizations consisted of quadrupling the total 1980 industrial and agricultural output value by the end of the century and of approaching the economic level of developed countries by the middle of the twenty-first century (Hu, 1982, and Zhao, 1987). This ambitious endeavor to transform the nation's comparatively backward economy called for and brought about a series of corresponding economic policy changes. Chief among them were the separation of ownership from managerial authority, the establishment of a market-oriented system, the promotion of horizontal ties in addition to the vertical leadership, the introduction of a macromanagement system based on indirect control of enterprises, and the development of an economy with plural ownership—state, collective and individual. In short, the highly centralized planning and control began to be replaced by more local, enterprise initiatives and a certain degree of market regulation (Zhao, 1987).

Undergirding the economic reform there emerged, as a gradual and cumulative process, the political restructuring which entailed the separation of authority of the CCP from the government, the delegation of power to localities, the granting of democracy, and the initiation of a comprehensive legal system. With the reform "the CCP relaxed its repressive controls and abandoned a revolutionary and mobilizational style of leadership for a more *laissez-faire* posture" (Falkenheim, 1989, p. 4). It was true that all the time the Four Cardinal Principles—the socialist road, the people's democratic dictatorship, the CCP leadership, and Marxism-Leninism-Mao Zedong thought—continued to be exhorted, but the political climate had been so relaxed and liberalized and the nation was so engrossed in the economic programs during the early and mid-1980s that these general and elusive political exhortations were more or less reduced to mere rhetoric, evoking little more than lip service.

All of these changes brought the crucial role of education into sharp focus and at the same time gave impetus to the educational reform that had been going on since 1978. To facilitate the rejuvenation of the nation's economy after the devastation of the Cultural Revolution, and more importantly, to promote the Four Modernizations, the training of large numbers of advanced specialized personnel was given top priority. Institutions of higher learning, which are "charged with the important task" (CCP, 1985) of such training, therefore, had to undergo corresponding changes to meet the challenges from the economic and political fronts. Fully aware of such urgent need, the CCP emphasized in its 1985 *Decision on the Reform of the Educational System* that:

> The key to success in the reform of the higher educational system ... is to change the management system of excessive government control over the institutions of higher learning, expand the powers of decision-making of the institutions of higher learning in school management ... and enable the institutions of higher learning to have the initiative and ability to meet the needs of economic and social development.

The Decision also suggested that institutional types be diversified, which meant that more three-year specialized colleges and two-year junior colleges should be set up in addition to the four- or five-year colleges or universities so as to better meet the need for different levels of skilled manpower. It was in this context that the management and structural reforms in Chinese higher education began to gain momentum and to yield concrete results.

The discussion of management reform in this chapter will begin with the autonomy that institutions of higher learning were granted and then, closely connected with it, the reinstitution of the president as chief executive officer. After dealing with these internal aspects of management reforms, this chapter will focus on the State Education Commission—its creation, functions and recentralization of power—as part of the external management change. The structural reform explored and reported in this chapter will be limited to the level and type, both of which had close links with the management reform.

Institutional Autonomy

The lessening of governmental control and the expansion of decision-making power made it possible for institutions of higher learning to have considerable autonomy in student enrollment, curriculum design, textbook selection, personnel management, funds disposal and international exchanges.

Prior to the 1980s, no students outside the mandated government plan could be admitted. With the autonomy resulting from the reform, students commissioned by enterprises and other government departments and students who were to pay tuition began to be enrolled on the premise that they pass the college entrance examinations and that the institutions of higher learning fulfill the quotas set by the central and provincial government authorities. This reform first benefitted the prospective students, the young and aspiring high school graduates. It provided them with more alternative channels for higher education at a traditional college or university. In a country with 1.84 college students per 1,000 people (UNESCO, 1988, p. 3/164), those who could have this opportunity were considered as fortunate as those enrolled under the unified government plan. They did not mind committing themselves, at this early stage, to a particular employer in a specific area. The contracts they had to sign with their sponsoring enterprises or government departments not only ensured them a job upon graduation, but also gave them a clear perspective of their career objectives. The tuition and incidental expenses those self-financed students had to pay were, no doubt, a burden for their families. But the passing of the college entrance examinations and gaining admission to a university was the envy of thousands of Chinese and naturally brought honor to the successful candidates and their families. And in a sociocultural milieu where higher education was imperative for those with any aspirations for social, political, or geographical mobility, the parents would not hesitate to secure, by all means, this second-best chance for their children. Money became a secondary concern. "We don't mind an austere life. So long as our son can get into a university we are prepared to make any sacrifices," a father said (Wang, 1989). Enterprises, corporations or government departments profitted from the modified enrollment system as well. The scarcity of college graduates in China made it a perennial struggle to recruit advanced specialized personnel. Now that there was the chance of securing their much-needed but hard-to-get talent for a small price, they were only too eager to become involved.

Institutions of higher learning were also beneficiaries of this arrangement. First, there was the financial concern—more students meant extra income. The payment from enterprises and tuition from self-financing students augmented the often insufficient government appropriations. The president of Northwest University, for example, disclosed that his university managed to obtain through commissioned training of students 30 million yuan of capital investment funds in a matter of three years, equivalent to the total investment by the provincial government in the previous 30 years. More important than the financial gains was the fuller use of existing facilities and faculty members. With the more than 2000 additional students admitted, the teacher-student ratio in the university was raised from 1:3 to 1:6.9, closer to the target set by the State Education Commission (1:8). Moreover, a number of new courses in engineering, management and law began to be offered in addition to the university's traditional courses in arts and sciences (Zhang, 1989).

Statistics of these employer-sponsored and self-paying students varied from institution to institution, place to place, and year to year. In Beijing, the nation's capital, it was reported that about 10 percent of the 1988 freshmen enrolled by universities and professional training institutions were paying their way (*CEN*, 1989, *17* (1), 24). Nationwide, over 25,000 employer-sponsored and 14,400 self-paying students were enrolled in 1987, 5 and 2.5 percent respectively of the year's total intake of students (Gao, 1988).

In addition to the autonomy in student enrollment, the reform gave institutions of higher learning the option to redesign academic programs in response to socioeconomic needs and to compile and select the textbooks for their programs. This put an end to the monopoly of the central Ministry of Education (later upgraded to the State Education Commission) over such matters. Though the national committees for syllabi, curricula and textbooks for all specialties were reactivated after the late 1970s, their main responsibility was to set national standards, not to enforce any mandatory adoption of the work they had produced. In other words, these committees were service-oriented quality-control mechanisms rather than all-powerful bodies issuing academic orders for mandatory implementation. The final decision as to what to choose or adopt rested with individual institutions. As observed by an informed China scholar, "teaching plans ... were drafted, but they are regarded as reference materials in contrast to the law-like status of the teaching plans of the fifties and sixties" (Hayhoe, 1989, p. 51). The writing and compiling of textbooks provided a good example. The manuscripts of the textbooks, generally several sets related to each discipline, were subjected to expert evaluation by these committees and their constituent subcommittees before being published. Whether the approved and published textbooks were selected for use by individual institutions was not the concern of the committees so long as the institution met certain nationally-mandated academic standards. The same was true of nationally designed and developed syllabi and curricula for all major specializations.

Another important effect from the lessening of governmental control was the allowance of institutions to make personnel decisions in the appointment and removal of vice presidents and other administrators below this level. In the early 1950s, college and university presidents and vice presidents were appointed by central government authorities above the Ministry of Education, but later these appointments were downgraded to the Ministry of Education or provincial governments. Middle-ranking institutional officials were likewise appointed by higher authorities. With the power further delegated as a consequence of the reform in the 1980s, only the presidents of a few nationally renowned and strategically important universities, such as Beijing University, were appointed by the State Council. The majority of presidents were appointed by the SEC or departments directly responsible for the institutions. The appointed presidents, in turn, nominated vice presidents as candidates for approval and appointment by the next higher authorities. And the presidents had the power to choose and appoint deans, department chairmen, and directors for research and administrative organizations of the university.

The same transformation held true for faculty promotion. During the 1950s and early 1960s, professorial positions had to be approved by the national Ministry of Education. With the newly gained personnel-management power, the authority to appoint such positions was given to provinces and even to some major universities.

The autonomy also enabled institutions of higher learning greater latitude in financial management. First, they were free to seek other sources of funding instead of relying on government appropriations alone. The alternative sources of funding included the income from extra students enrolled, as already reported, remuneration from contracted research, loans from the World Bank, and donations from enterprises and individuals at home and from organizations and individuals overseas. As was facetiously analogized, institutions of higher learning began to be fed by "a hundred families" in addition to the "imperial bestowal." By aggressively exploring every possible avenue, institutions of higher learning generated substantial funds, alleviating the burden of the state and supplementing the government appropriations, which often fell short of their needs. A survey conducted in 1988 revealed that owing to price increases, universities experienced serious deficits. Allocations from the government could only cover two-thirds of the operating expenses (Johnson, 1989). The income from other channels became an indispensable supplementary source which often helped universities tide over crises. At some nationally renowned institutions of higher learning, the extra income constituted a substantial proportion of the total operating budget. In 1987 Beijing University generated, through much ingenuity, 50 percent of its income (Wang, 1987). Beijing Normal University and Tongji University in Shanghai reported similar percentages of funds obtained by alternative means (Lin, 1989, and Xiao, 1988). In Tianjin, Nankai University's newly established School of Economics raised 21 million yuan for a new economics complex. In contrast, the total capital construction budget for the entire university for five years (1986-1990) was only 30 million yuan (Johnson, 1989).

Besides the freedom to seek alternative sources of income and to engage in money-making endeavors, institutions of higher learning were also allowed to dispose of funds (whether appropriated by the government or self-generated) at their own discretion. No funds outside the government allocation and no carryover from the previous fiscal year had to be turned over to higher authorities. No expenditure for a building or its design had to be submitted for examination and approval by a higher authority in charge. Much of the auditing red tape was also cut (Wang, 1987). Most noticeable of all among the newly gained autonomies in institutional management was the freedom to conduct scholarly and academic exchanges with overseas universities. Before the late 1970s, when China was closed to the outside world and individual contact with Western nations was restricted and suspect, academic exchange with other countries was invariably arranged by the government. No individuals or institutions could or dared tread this highly sensitive and even dangerous ground. With many of the restrictions eliminated and much of the fear allayed following China's open-door policy, academic and scholarly exchanges with foreign countries, especially the industrialized nations, had developed by the late 1980s to such an extent that there was hardly any four-year Chinese college or university which did not send its faculty members or students overseas for advanced studies, nor any major university campus in China which did not have foreign professors engaging in teaching or research and foreign students studying Chinese or pursuing higher degrees in various disciplines (Zhao, 1989). By 1987 Beijing University had signed educational and academic agreements with 50 universities in many parts of the world (Wang, 1987). A specialized college with a student body of 1500 maintained scholarly and academic exchanges with 15 overseas colleges and universities (Sun, 1989).

All these newly acquired decision-making powers, in areas such as student enrollment, curriculum design, personnel management, fund disposal and international exchange—often taken for granted in the West—marked a new stage in Chinese university management. A macrocontrol mechanism with indirect regulation began to be practiced in place of the enforcement of specific rules and regulations and the overseeing of the day-to-day operation of institutional affairs. In other words, the SEC began to direct and coordinate the nation's higher education as a whole instead of supervising individual institutions of higher learning, as it had been doing for years. This reform measure transformed institutions of higher learning from government "appendages" to relatively independent educational entities and, more importantly, released their enthusiasm and initiative in contributing to the nation's social and economic development. No longer tightly bound by government regulations, institutions of higher learning began mapping out their own futures instead of waiting passively for mandates from above. For example, Lu Yongxiang, the charismatic president of Zhejiang University, proclaimed that their faculty and staff would make every effort to build the university by the year 2000 into a first-rate university in China, a university with international recognition (1989). In fact, many of the significant scientific findings by the university faculty, the international symposiums and seminars sponsored by the university, and the well-equipped laboratories open to the public as well as to the university faculty and students had already earned the university a name not only in China but also in the world (President's Office, 1988).

The Reinstatement of the President as
Chief Executive Officer

While all these autonomies were highly desirable and welcomed, another problem had to be resolved. Though many of the external government restrictions and intrusions were beginning to be removed, the university president was not automatically given a free hand in administering institutional affairs. There still existed, at the internal level, the all-powerful CCP university committee (CCPUC) to which the president was required to subject himself for leadership and to submit for approval decisions, if any, he was in a position to make. Unless a satisfactory solution was reached in the president vis-à-vis CCPUC relationship, no university could possibly take full advantage of the precious autonomies they had gained.

Aware of the problem, the SEC revived, on a trial basis in 1985, what was officially termed "the president responsibility system," whereby the president was again to function as the chief executive officer in institutional management as he had done in the early 1950s. No longer was it necessary or required for him to go through the CCPUC for many major decisions he was to make. Broadly speaking, this reform measure was derived from the political restructuring going on nationwide—the separation of power from the CCP and government. Within an institution of higher learning, this entailed the transfer of managing authority from the chairman of CCPUC to the president, who might or might not be a member of the CCP, but was almost universally selected and appointed from among the intellectual community, not the CCP bureaucracy. The renewed practice ushered in a new stage in the internal governance pattern of institutions of higher learning.

The revival of this system followed an inconsistent past in which the internal university governance in China had experienced different forms responding to different political climates at different times. During the early 1950s when the rehabilitation of the economy, which was at the brink of collapse due to civil war and foreign plunder, was the overriding concern of the nation and hence the training of a large contingent of specialized personnel became essential, university management was largely left in the hands of the intellectuals who had the ability and the expertise to organize teaching and research. But beginning in the late 1950s when education was made to serve primarily CCP politics, intellectuals, who had been a suspect class and had to go through "ideological remolding" to prove their worth, could no longer be entrusted with the responsibility. From the late 1950s till the promulgation of the *CCP Decision on the Reform of the Educational System* in 1985, various internal governance structures were evolved. But no matter what the pattern was, it was the CCPUC which had the power to override the president and had the final say in institutional management, both administrative and academic (Wu, 1988). In this case, the checks and balances for university presidents were twofold. Apart from policies mandated from the top down for implementation, there was an overseer at hand monitoring every move the president made and ensuring that he did everything right. Under these circumstances, university presidents found it hard even to act as effective and efficient managers, to say nothing of functioning as inspiring instructional leaders.

However, when the political climate changed and the importance of higher education to the nation's economic development was reaffirmed, reform in the internal university governance structure became imperative. From 1985 on, the president responsibility system began to be revived in 103 colleges and universities, about 10 percent of the total number (Zhu, 1988). The major authority and responsibility of the president came to include decision-making for all institutional affairs (except those related to the CCPUC) with specifically delegated power over teaching, research, personnel, budgeting, faculty promotion and institutional exchanges with foreign countries.

With the presidents in charge of both curriculum and administration, the function of the CCPUC became supervisory—conducting investigations and political and moral education, assisting the president in his duties, disciplining CCP members, and ensuring the implementation of the CCP line and policies (Lu, 1989). Their role was to help, not to interfere, with the exercising of the managerial power of the president. What all this signified was that the intellectuals began to be seen as part of the working class vital for the nation's drive toward the Four Modernizations. They were no longer distrusted as an alien force hostile or pernicious to the Communist leadership.

This revival of the president's overall control of institutional affairs, however, did not mean the disappearance of all checks and balances for the president. It was true that the CCPUC became much less visible, but it continued to exist, functioning as leader. Moreover, as a major shift in institutional management, the president responsibility system had not yet become universal. In most of China's 1075 colleges and universities, the CCPUC remained the final decision-maker, and the possibility of a complete switchover was still remote. In a speech in 1988, Zhu Kaixuan, a leading member of the SEC, cautioned that the system was still at a field-testing stage and admonished the other institutions of higher learning not to "rush into" it before conditions were ripe. When or if the whole changeover would take place depended largely on how the political pendulum would swing in the near future.

Although the increases in the president's responsibility and autonomy were still limited to a minority of institutions of higher learning, the departmental level of authority had been put into the hands of the department chairman throughout the higher education system. Before the 1980s the department chairman had to work under the department's CCP general branch, which passed final decisions on such matters as faculty pay raise and promotion and student job assignment. Teaching and research plans had to be submitted for the CCP branch approval before the chairman could put them into practice. Appointed by and responsible to the president after the late 1970s, the chairman of the department could bypass the departmental CCP organization in all aspects of the department management. As at the university level, the CCP organization still existed, but its function was likewise downgraded into a supervisory one.

The State Education Commission (SEC)

All the autonomies granted to individual institutions and the managerial authority granted to the president did not mean the demise of the central-level administration for higher education. So instead of abolishing the Ministry of Education, the CCP decided to set up an even higher administrative organ to better guide the overall educational development and to more effectively sustain the momentum of the reform movement than before. This presented an interesting but understandable paradox. On the one hand, there was the decentralization with much of the decision-making power delegated to local levels and institutions. On the other hand, there was the upgrading of power and a certain degree of recentralization at the central level.

Created in 1985, the SEC was decreed as the supreme administrative authority for the education system in China (SEC, 1989, p. 36). With the same rank as other central ministries which ran their own institutions of higher learning, the former Ministry of Education had found it difficult to lead and coordinate higher education and its reforms. The State Education Commission, which was directly under the State Council, had a much broader scope of power than its predecessor and thus a greater ability to oversee and facilitate the nation's educational development. Befitting its higher status, the then Vice Premier of the State Council, Li Peng, was appointed Chairman of the Commission. Other members of the leading body included not only a number of full-time vice ministers in charge, but also vice ministers from other central ministries and commissions under the State Council (SEC, 1988, p. 20).

In keeping with its elevated status, the SEC's main responsibilities were to formulate policies and guiding principles, forecast future needs, work out overall plans, coordinate the efforts of different departments of education and provide unified direction and guidance for educational reform endeavors

(SEC, 1988, p. 20). But in exercising these responsibilities, the SEC would focus its work on macro- instead of micromanagement in line with the main thrust of the reforms at political and economic fronts.

To streamline the nationwide administrative system, provinces, autonomous regions and municipalities directly under the central government were requested to set up corresponding education commissions in place of the local education departments (Zhu, 1988). The upgrading of the central administrative organ in charge of education was to be paralleled at provincial levels.

With the establishment of the education commissions at the central and provincial levels, the external management hierarchy of Chinese higher education became three-tiered: at the top, there was the State Education Commission; in the middle, there were the education commissions of the provinces, autonomous regions or municipalities, and at the bottom, major cities or prefectures under provincial-level governments. Interspersed among these levels were educational departments under central government ministries which exercised leadership over institutions of higher learning under their sponsorship. This management structure classified the Chinese institutions of higher learning into the following four categories:

1) The 36 institutions directly under the State Education Commission. All of these institutions were national-level colleges or universities except four of the six teacher-training universities, one in each of China's geographical regions. Many of them were multidisciplined, prestigious, pacesetting institutions with both undergraduate and graduate programs, such as the nationally renowned and internationally known Beijing University, Qinghua University and Fudan University. Out of the 36 colleges or universities, 25 were among the key institutions, which will be discussed later.

2) Institutions under the central ministries. Colleges and universities in this category were generally specialized with the purpose of training advanced personnel for the sponsoring ministries and their constituent enterprises or corporations. Most of them were geared to nationwide needs and had undergraduate as well as graduate programs. Some of them were among the nation's key colleges or universities.

3) Institutions under the provinces, autonomous regions and municipalities. These locally-oriented institutions, consisting of multidisciplined universities, teacher training schools, and specialized colleges, formed the bulk of Chinese institutions of higher learning.

Most of them were four-year institutions with both undergraduate and graduate programs.

4) Institutions under major cities. Institutions of this category were mostly newly established junior colleges offering two- to three-year technical and vocational training programs. This was the fastest growing sector of Chinese higher education, the one in which most of the future student growth could be expected to take place.

Underlying this fairly generalized classification by line of authority, there existed a clear hierarchy of prestige and status. For Chinese colleges and universities, it was often not what an institution was doing or had accomplished, but rather where it belonged that was crucially important. The higher an institution's line of authority was, the more visible it became, and with the visibility came the privileges—appropriations, capital investment, research projects and funds, priority for nationwide student selection and opportunities for government-sponsored international exchange programs. In a sense, this status hierarchy and the privileges along with it were historical rather than man-made—the present nationally renowned institutions had been of national caliber for decades, and their status had been taken for granted. But what the SEC did upon its creation was to continue this hierarchical structure by assuming direct jurisdiction over those already better-endowed, better-staffed, and hence better-known institutions, 36 in all, while leaving the majority of colleges and universities to the care of local authorities, thus consolidating and making official the already superior position of these few institutions.

Key Institutions and the Pyramid

Besides placing these 36 institutions under its direct administration, the SEC also inherited and continued to concentrate resources on the 96 key colleges and universities designated by its predecessor in 1978 and 1979 (CIER, 1983, p. 150). Out of the 96 priority institutions ten were singled out for even greater investment—an additional 100 million yuan from the state (Lin, 1989, and Rosen, 1985). If Chinese higher education was developing in the shape of a pyramid, these key institutions and the league of the key institutions formed the pinnacle. What the reform had brought for these institutions, which were entrusted with most advanced research projects and the training of world-class scholars, was not only institutional autonomy like every other institution, but also a high degree of recentralization, which for them meant nothing but benefits. If the recentralization was seen as government intrusion, it was a welcome one. Here perhaps autonomy and recentralization did not conflict with each other.

This recentralization of the external management and nonequivalent distribution of resources perpetuated an elite sector among Chinese institutions of higher learning, which were already training a tiny elite section of the Chinese population. But in a country with an acute shortage of resources (the per capita GNP in 1988, for instance, was only about US$ 350), this practice was justifiable. "All countries eventually abandon the principle of equality in higher education in order to concentrate students, staff and facilities in centers of excellence, because of the costs involved in scattering them among all institutions of higher learning" (World Bank, 1985, p. 125). Also, in a country with as diverse a system of higher education as China, it was imperative to have a few bellwethers to set academic standards.

Structural Reform—Diversification by Level and Type

Until the recent reforms Chinese higher education had been plagued by another problem besides rigid government control. For over 30 years, efforts had been mostly concentrated on the unitary four- to five-year undergraduate programs. Graduate education and junior college courses had received little attention and had developed at a very slow pace, resulting in a disproportionate supply of much-needed high-level manpower and at the same time a grave waste of talent.

Graduate studies, which had been a fledgling enterprise from 1949 to 1965, came to a full stop for 12 years during and after the Cultural Revolution. The 32,400 graduate students trained before 1965 fell far short of the need for teachers, researchers and scientists of a high caliber in the nation's social and economic development (SEC, 1989, p. 110). A 1983 World Bank study showed that among faculty members in 20 key universities, only 7.8 percent had completed graduate work at the master's level (p. 168). Except for a very small number of old professors who had studied in industrialized countries, almost no faculty member had doctoral degrees.

Restored in 1978, graduate programs in China developed rapidly in the 1980s. Statistics disclosed by the SEC revealed that from 1978 to 1987, 200,000 graduate students were enrolled in China's institutions of higher learning and research organizations. Of those enrolled, 70,000 had completed their studies by 1988 (1989, p. 110).

The reinvigorated graduate education in China had two levels—master's and doctorate—and three types of students—doctoral, master's and non-degree. The length of study for master's students was two to three years (with a trend to reduce it to two) and three years for doctorates. Overall policies on the enrollment, programs and job assignment were the responsibility of the SEC. Province-level educational commissions took charge of the management of graduate students in their respective regions under the general guidelines formulated and mandated from the SEC. A national committee made up of noted scholars in different fields of study was authorized to accredit institutions for graduate programs and individuals as advisors for doctoral students. Table 3.1 provides some statistical information about graduate studies in China in 1987.

The structural imbalance was also reflected in the two- to three-year short-cycle programs offered at some four-year colleges and universities and at junior colleges. In 1978, the ratio of students enrolled for these short-cycle programs compared to the four- or five-year programs was 0.37:1 (Li, 1988). But what China needs during the remaining years of this century for its social and economic development, according to Wang Yibing (1985), a fellow of the Policy Research Office of the SEC, is an equal number of graduates from the two categories of programs. A major study co-chaired by a SEC official in charge of education development and policy research and the director of Beijing University's Institute of Higher Education also disclosed that for 17 out of the 33 years between 1947 and 1981, students in these short-cycle courses made up no more than 10 percent of the total college and university enrollment (Hao and Wang, 1987, p. 19). The end result was that in many cases university graduates had to do the work that could be done as well or even better by middle-level technicians trained at the junior college level.

This problem of imbalance was also discussed by other scholars and the World Bank. Long (1989) stated that the overwhelming majority of China's 500,000 state-owned enterprises were medium and small in size, engaging in the manufacturing of products with finalized designs. What they needed most were specially trained technicians who did not have to undertake four or five years of university education. In its *Country Study* series, the World Bank (1986, p. 29) concluded that short-cycle courses offered at colleges and universities or specialized junior colleges could, with about half the investment and at a much faster speed, satisfy the most pressing demand of China's social and economic development. Based on these studies and pressured by the actual need of these enterprises and the fast-burgeoning township industries—1.5 million in all—for even more technical manpower (Long, 1989), the CCP called the attention of the whole nation to coordinate

Table 2.1

Graduate Studies in China in 1987

	TOTAL	INSTITUTION	CAS*	CASS*	MINISTRY*	PROVINCE*
Institutions	755	408	113	1	117	56
Students	120,191	106,185	6,309	781	5,970	946
PhD	8,969	7,319	1,230	149	267	4
Master's	104,483	92,251	5,041	632	5,617	942
Nondegree	6,739	6,615	38	86		
Advisors						
PhD	3,208	2,488	489	74	154	3
Master's	43,604	35,624	3,082	297	3,862	559
Nondegree	563	563				

* CAS: the Chinese Academy of Sciences
* CASS: the Chinese Academy of Social Sciences
* Ministry: research organizations of central ministries
* Province: research organizations at the provincial level

Source: 3rd Department, SEC, 1988. *Post-Secondary Education in China: Present State and Trends*. Beijing: State Education Commission (SEC), p. 11.

with the government in consciously readjusting and reforming the structure of higher education, changing the irrational ratio of engineers and technicians, and making every effort to accelerate the development of short-cycle courses which were capable of producing the much-needed technical manpower at a faster and more economical speed. As a matter of fact, administrative measures had been taken as early as the late 1970s to correct this imbalance. In 1987, these short-cycle specialized colleges had increased from 190 in 1982 to 468 in number with a corresponding growth of enrollment from 84,000 to 284,000, at the rate of 266 and 340 percent respectively (Long, 1989).

Parallel with the development of these junior colleges, which were part of the mainstream institutions of higher learning with everything—tuition, residence and job allocation—taken care of by the government, there emerged the American-type community colleges, whose students had to commute to classes, pay tuition and find employment by themselves upon graduation. Geared to local needs, these colleges, 122 in all by the 1987 statistics, offered courses in 217 disciplines, including management, service, finance and economics, applied humanities, political science and law, medicine, agriculture and forestry (3rd Department, SEC, 1988, p. 20). Their students were enrolled from among higher school graduates who had passed the national college entrance examinations, but with slightly lower marks than those selected by traditional colleges and universities, and from secondary vocational and technical schools. The length of study ranged between two and three years, and before graduation students sat for a standard examination organized by the state (3rd Department, SEC, p. 21). The rate of employment for the graduates from these community colleges was virtually 100 percent (World Bank, 1986, p. 14). If China would not, in the immediate future, establish new four-year institutions of higher learning because of her limited resources, it will be in this type of college that the future increases in student population could be expected to take place.

The initial correction of the disproportionate ratio of different levels of higher education and the impressive growth in enrollment, however, still fell far short of China's need for advanced, special high- and middle-level manpower to fulfill its ambitious plans of quadrupling the gross value of industrial and agricultural output by the year 2000 and of standing among the front rank of major world powers by the middle of the twenty-first century. In its study in collaboration with the Chinese SEC, the World Bank (1986) concluded that a balanced number of 22.3 million college graduates would be needed if China were to realize these objectives. To meet this manpower demand, the entire system of [Chinese] higher eduction would need to   grow by a factor of five. A strategy in pursuit of this goal would necessarily follow three tracks: (a) sharp increase in enrollment in existing institutions; (b) establishment of new institutions; and (c) expansion of nonconventional approaches to higher education [p. 10].

Out of the three solutions suggested by the World Bank, the first two solutions were not yet practicable due to China's limited capacity for educational investment. The budget for education had been fluctuating between 2 and 3 percent of the nation's GNP, far below 4.5 to 5 percent, which was the average education spending in the world (Li, 1989). And the annual 15 percent increase in government appropriations over the past few years had been wiped out by inflation and price hikes (Li). Inherent problems, such as the self-containment with residences for all students free of charge and staff/faculty at nominal rent and the related expenditures, also incurred extra costs and hence added to the difficulty in the expansion of enrollment. Setting up new institutions would be more costly than tapping the potential of the existing ones and had, therefore, been ruled out by the authorities. The only viable alternative left open was to further diversify the types of institutions. This meant, in China's case, to expand the already fast-developing nontraditional adult institutions of higher learning, which cost seven to ten times less per student than traditional colleges and universities (World Bank, 1986, p. 29) and encourage and permit social groups and individuals to run schools as well.

Adult institutions of higher learning in China during the 1980s fell into the following categories: 1) the TV university; 2) staff/worker university; 3) farmer university; 4) colleges for management personnel; 5) colleges for teachers and educational administrators; 6) independent correspondence courses and 7) correspondence courses and night schools run by traditional colleges and universities. The number of these institutions with their enrollment and teachers is tabulated in Table 2.2.

Of these adult institutions of higher learning in China the most significant was the TV university, in terms of both the enrollment and the scope of course offerings. Established in 1960, closed during the Cultural Revolution but reopened in 1979, it consisted of a network extending from the Central TV University in Beijing to 39 TV colleges at the provincial level with 497 branches, 1550 stations and 2700 classes (*Guangming Daily*, 1989, October 24, p. 1). In all parts of the country, classes in about 400 short-cycle disciplines ranging from science and engineering, liberal arts, management, and agricultural sciences were on-air on a special color TV channel every day at fixed times, catering to the varying time schedules of different students. In addition to the regular telecast, a special satellite channel had started in 1986 to beam on a daily basis from 4:30 to 11:30 p.m. over a nationwide network of ground satellite receiving stations with a capacity of 4000 hours of telecourses a year. Apart from these programs from the Central TV University, which made up 60 percent of the total, provincial-level TV colleges produced programs on their own to meet specific local needs (Xiao, 1989).

All the TV university programs were geared to vocational and technical training in the much-needed areas specified above. Full-time students came from two sources: high school graduates who had passed college entrance examinations, but did not score high enough marks to ensure them a place

Table 2.2

Adult Institutions of Higher Learning in China in 1987:
Numbers, Enrollment and Teachers

Institution	Number	Enrollment	Teacher
TV univ.	39	566,000	9,100
Staff/worker univ.	915	338,000	36,300
Farmer univ.	5	1,104	200
Management pers. coll.	168	55,000	13,622
Educational coll.	268	251,200	24,900
Ind. corr. courses	4	33,300	200
Corr. course & night by coll. & univ.	600*	612,000	
TOTAL	**1,399**	**1,860,000**	**84,300**

* Not included in the total number of adult institutions of higher learning.

Sources: State Education commission (SEC), 1988. *Education in China*. Beijing: State Education commission, pp. 83-90.
3rd Department, SEC, 1988. *Post-Secondary Education in China: Present State and Trends*. Beijing: State Education commission, p. 5.
Yi, Nong. (1988, June). Lunlianhe juban chengren gaodeng jiaoyu [On combined efforts in running adult higher education]. *Zhongguo Gaodeng Jiaoyu [Chinese Higher Education]*, pp. 40-41.

at traditional colleges and universities, and people with high school diplomas who had been employed for over two years. The latter had to seek the approval of their employers because their study was on a leave-of-absence basis with full pay and retained tenure. The courses were, by their nature, open to part-time and spare-time students. With the rigid academic-year system replaced by credit hours, the length of study was flexible. Students could graduate at any time so long as they passed the required exams. Since its reopening, the TV university had trained 1.05 million fully accredited graduates, 40 percent of the total number of traditional college and university graduates during the same period, and 90 percent of the total number of graduates from all the other adult institutions of higher learning. In other words, 22 out of 100 college and university graduates in China over recent years came from the TV university (Guangming Daily, October 24, 1989, p. 1).

This massive quantity, however, was not achieved at the expense of quality. A survey of 320,000 TV university graduates revealed that employers were highly satisfied with the expertise, managerial ability and foreign-language competency of the TV university graduates. According to the survey, these graduates made up an indispensable backbone force of skilled manpower for different walks of life. Many had distinguished themselves in their fields of work. Facts proved that TV university education provided an effective means for special manpower development with particular relevance to remote, rural and ethnic minority areas (*Guangming Daily*, October 24, 1989, p. 1).

As with traditional colleges and universities, the TV university and all its branch colleges were under a three-tiered leadership—central, provincial, local (city or prefecture), but they were more fortunate than many traditional colleges and universities in that they were heavily subsidized by the World Bank loans.

Smaller in scale, but similarly widespread as the TV university, adult institutions of higher learning for staff and workers were established and administered mainly by enterprises in almost all parts of the country (SEC, 1989, p. 23). The vast majority of the 500 specialized courses they offered were short-cycle ones dictated by the needs of the sponsoring enterprises. Practical abilities were emphasized in teaching. Students at these institutions were drawn from the enterprises for full-time, part-time and spare-time studies for a correspondingly variable length of time. For those engaged in full-time study, three years were required, and for the part-timers, four or five years. Upon completing their programs, students returned to work for their sponsoring enterprises, factories or companies.

Alongside the universities for staff and workers, universities for farmers were also promoted. Run by local governments, these universities offered two- or three-year full-time college-level courses to train technicians who had some experience with agriculture, forestry, animal husbandry and fishery for more advanced work in these fields. As it was at an experimental stage, this type of adult higher education was significantly small as compared with other forms, as shown in Table 2.3.

Another form of adult institution of higher learning was the management personnel college. Administered by central or local governments, these colleges offered two- or three-year courses to those with practical experience in the management of different industries. Owing to the pressing demand for more and better management personnel, this type of full-time adult higher education developed at a very fast pace. From 1983 to 1987, the number of

Table 2.3

Traditional and Nontraditional Chinese Institutions of Higher Learning
in 1987: A Comparison

TYPE	INSTITUTIONS	ENROLLMENT (million)	FACULTY
Traditional	1,063	2.06	385,400
Nontraditional	1,399	1.86	84,300

Source: State Education Commission (SEC), 1988. *A Survey of Education in China.*
Beijing: State Education Commission, p. 2.

these colleges increased from 15 to 168, and the faculty had grown from 800 to 13,600 (SEC, 1989, p. 94).

Greater in number than management personnel colleges were educational colleges. Administered by educational departments at provincial or major city levels, these colleges aimed at training teachers and administrators of secondary schools. After two years of full-time study or refresher courses, these trainees returned to their former schools or educational administrative organs. Besides teaching, these colleges also undertook such missions as research in educational theories, supervision in teaching and the development of teaching materials.

In addition to these colleges and universities, adult higher education was also made available in two correspondence forms: independent correspondence courses and correspondence courses run by traditional colleges and universities. The difference between these two forms of courses was that the former was organized and administered for a more restricted student body by ministries under the State Council and local government agencies for education, while the latter was offered for a wider audience by traditional colleges and universities in disciplines where high demand was dictated by the society at large. Taking advantage of the autonomy they had gained and making full use of their faculty, colleges and universities also operated evening schools for part-time studies for those who had, for various reasons, been denied a chance for regular college education but now felt the urgent need of it, either for their current work or for personal advancement. Since the late 1970s, both the correspondence and evening education programs had expanded as rapidly as traditional higher education and were surpassed in rate of growth only by the TV university system.

With their flexibility and phenomenal growth, these institutions of adult higher learning constituted a sizable supplement of Chinese higher education (see Table 2.3). The whole system was, in the words of the World Bank,

> probably the best and most comprehensive in the developing world, and it should continue to be a very important factor in China's human resource development. It should be used to meet many urgent manpower needs in industry, agriculture, education and other sectors of Chinese society. [1983, p. 176]

In addition to these types of institutions with formal instruction or tutorial in classrooms, China developed from the early 1980s government-organized college-level examinations for those studying by themselves. The examinations were administered by provincial-level committees set up specifically for that purpose. Held at regular intervals, these examinations covered over 70 fields of study pertinent to local needs. To help the candidates with the examinations in their chosen fields of study, guidelines and requested and suggested reading lists were distributed in newsletter form by the committees in collaboration with colleges and universities in the locality which were called upon to draft the examination questions and mark the examination papers. The examinations for the self-taught were open to all citizens regardless of age and previous schooling. The on-the-job candidates who passed the examinations might be transferred to a new job which would put what they had learned to use. Thus, successful candidates who had not had a job would stand a better chance for employment. Since 1981 when the system began, 3.5 million people had taken the examinations. Of these, 140,000 passed junior college requirements, 150 were qualified as traditional four-year college graduates and 2.1 million were awarded single-subject qualification certificates (Wang Jiping, 1988).

The diversification of institutional types took other forms as well. While the adult institutions of higher learning and examinations for the self-taught were both controlled and funded by public expenses, private colleges and universities, which had been banned since 1949, had appeared one after another at no cost to the government. Seventeen such colleges were reported to have been set up in Beijing since 1982 (Fu and Yang, 1989). In Shantou, a seaport along China's south coast, a new university financed by the well-known Hong Kong businessman Li Ke-shing boasted 12 departments in liberal arts, science, engineering, medicine, law, business and art design. The university's 550 faculty members were drawn from other Chinese colleges and universities, 26 percent of whom were professors and associate professors (*People's Daily,* Overseas Edition, February 5, 1990, p. 4). In Shanghai, five years of painstaking effort saw a private school develop into a sizable college with 17,000 students and nine departments. For his initiative and contribution, the founder, a retired teacher, was honored as an outstanding educator and elected a member of the Chinese People's Political Consultative Committee. Encouraged and helped by all sides, including U.S. and Canadian universities, the educator set about upgrading his college into a private university (Ji, 1989).

Foreigners, too, were allowed and assisted to set up educational establishments in collaboration with Chinese authorities. In the central province of Henan, a secluded 170-acre former retreat for the top CCP and government leadership became, in 1985, the campus of the Huanghe (the Yellow River) University—a brand-new institution of higher learning with an 18-member board of directors made up of nine local Chinese officials and nine Chinese Americans. In place of the CCPUC, the board formulated basic policies for institutional affairs while the president, nominated by the board and appointed by the provincial government, was entrusted with the responsibility of the management. Courses offered by the university included economic management, computer science, American studies and English literature—all conducted by a joint faculty of Chinese and Americans. Though the university, a kind of joint venture in education, had a long way to go to establish itself, its opening and operation marked a new page in the development of Chinese higher education (Han, 1989).

Summary

The ongoing political and economic restructuring in China during the late 1970s and early 1980s ensured and expedited reforms in higher education management and structure. Significant among the management reforms was the expansion of the decision-making power of institutions of higher learning. Instead of being subject to rigid control by central authorities as before, institutions of higher learning began to enjoy considerable autonomy in student enrollment, curriculum design, textbook selection, personnel management, fund disposal and international exchange. Another important aspect of the management reform concerned the university president, who was restored as chief executive officer of institutional affairs. With the president assuming primary responsibility, the formerly all powerful CCPUC was shifted to a supervisory role. Though it was limited to 10 percent of colleges and universities, this reintroduction of the president responsibility system marked a significant change in the internal governance pattern, which was a measure in keeping with political and economic reforms across the country.

In contrast to the internal management reform with the resultant autonomies for institutions of higher learning and the decision-making power for the president, there was, externally, the strengthening of the CCP and government leadership over education through the establishment of the State Education Commission, which had a much broader scope of power than its predecessor, the Ministry of Education. The mission of this central government agency with its elevated status was to formulate general guidelines and overall plans, coordinate all government agencies' work concerning education and make unified arrangements for the reform of the entire education system.

Executing these macrostructural tasks, the SEC left the administration of the overwhelming majority of institutions of higher learning in the hands of central government ministries, provincial-level authorities and major cities. However, the SEC had 36 colleges and universities under its direct jurisdiction and designated 96 institutions of higher learning (including 25 of the 36 under its direct administration) as key colleges and universities which were granted priority in resource allocation and student selection. Whether this practice was defensible or not did not matter in terms of China's university management, but what could be said was that, paradoxically, the more prestigious an institution of higher learning was, the more autonomy it enjoyed, and hence the more innovative it tended to be. These 36 and 96 institutions were, no doubt, prestigious colleges and universities in China's higher education system.

In addition to the management change, this chapter dealt with the development of institutional level and type. The institutional level was mainly concerned with graduate education and junior and community colleges, the two areas which had been largely ignored before the 1980s. The reform efforts in the 1980s brought about notable achievements in these two programs, which began to correct the imbalance in the supply of different levels of manpower for China's modernization drive.

Of particular significance with respect to the institutional level was the appearance of the American-type community colleges, an entirely new phenomenon in Chinese higher education. Though outside the mainstream of Chinese colleges and universities, these colleges were responsive to social needs and had great potential for future increases in number and in student enrollment.

The discussion of the institutional type concentrated on the impressive development of the nontraditional institutions of higher learning for adults, which became an indispensable aspect of Chinese higher education in meeting the nation's growing need for skilled manpower. With highly flexible curricula and much reduced cost, these institutions not only provided a practical alternative for higher education, but also showed great vitality for future development.

In addition to focusing on the institutions of adult education, this chapter briefly discussed private colleges and universities, which were banned when the PRC was established. In the markedly changed political and economic context, private institutions established by individuals and social organizations began to appear. It is difficult to predict how long this trend would be sustained, but like the various categories of adult higher institutions of learning, these private colleges and universities helped to meet a significant need.

3

Curriculum and Instruction

Problems inherent in Chinese higher education were many and multifaceted. In addition to the excessive central government control and the disproportion between the two- to three-year short-cycle and four- or five-year full-cycle curricular structure, Chinese higher education was beleaguered by a number of other deficiencies. Outstanding among them were the lopsidedness in major fields of study, the overspecialization of undergraduates, the narrow scope of course offerings and the outmoded methods of instruction. All of these problems were identified in the 1985 *CCP Decision on the Reform of the Educational System* as obstacles to the building of a viable higher education system compatible with the deepening of the political and economic reforms and conducive to the realization of the modernization goals. Through government readjustment policies, institutional efforts and market regulation over recent years, these long-standing problems began to be resolved.

Correcting Curricular Imbalance

While expanding the enrollment of students in sciences and engineering before the late 1970s, China had neglected the growth in other areas, particularly in such fields as political science, law, finance and economics. As illustrated in Tables 3.1, 3.2 and 3.3, there were only two institutions specializing in political science and law out of a total number of 598 colleges and universities in 1978. And most of the comprehensive universities which had departments of economics or political science did not resume student enrollment in these programs until the early 1980s. Because of the neglect, the number of students majoring in political science and law only accounted for 0.2 percent of the entire college student enrollment at the time. The situation with finance and economics was not any better. In 1978, the' institutions specializing in these fields of study merely made up 3.5 percent of the total, the number of specializations 5 percent, and the enrollment 2.1 percent. The imbalance was further evidenced by a comparison of the rate of increase in graduates from major fields of study in 1949 and 1984. While the total number of graduates in 1984 was 24 times that of 1949, with engineering multiplying 48 times, medicine and pharmacology 59 and teacher training 54 times respectively, the graduates from finance and economics showed only a modest growth of 8 times. In sharp contrast to all these increases, graduates in political science and law dropped by 30 percent (Hao and Zhang, p. 9).

Naturally, the comparatively small growth in finance and economics and the decrease in political science and law failed to satisfy the urgent demand for the personnel expert in these fields for the nation's social and economic development. Statistics showed that the 42,000 students enrolled in finance and economics from 1981 to 1985 could only average about one for each of the over 400,000 enterprises in the whole of the country, which would be inadequate even if all the graduates were assigned to work in these enterprises. The discrepancy between the supply and demand was even greater in the fields of political science and law. From these fields of study, there were only 8,400 graduates from 1981 to 1985. But in China, the courts and procuratorates above the county level alone numbered over 12,000 (Cai and Zhao, 1987).

This serious problem of discrepancy began to be addressed in the reform movement. Under the auspices of the MOE and later SEC, a series of national and regional conferences was held to discuss the problems and to work out possible solutions. Following the conferences, all the institutions of political science and law and of finance and economics were reopened one by one. The People's University in Beijing, which was the nation's most prestigious institution in these fields, began again to take the position of leadership. The greater momentum of the reform in the mid-1980s and, more importantly, the 1985 *CCP Decision,* which specifically singled out these fields for a more accelerated development, further promoted the increase in the number of institutions and specializations in these fields of study and training. By 1988, the number of colleges and universities specializing in political science and law increased to 25, which was 12.5 times the 1978 figure. The enrollment grew over 80 times and the number of specializations four times over 1978. Though not as phenomenal as the growth in political science and law, the number of institutions, the enrollment figures and the type of specializations available in finance and economics also registered notable increases. Compared with 1978, the number of institutions and the figure of enrollment in 1988 multiplied, respectively, 3.5 and 5 times. By way of comparison, the overall number of institutions of higher learning in China increased by about 95 percent and the total enrollment increased 134 percent during the same period. The type of specializations, despite repeated regrouping and amalgamation, remained more or less unchanged (see Tables 3.1, 3.2 and 3.3; MOE, 1985, p. 54; *Guangming Daily,* September 22, 1989, p. 2).

In spite of the impressive growth resulting from the readjustment measures taken in the early and middle 1980s, the training of advanced, skilled people in these fields still fell far short of the demand. The northeastern province of Jilin provided a good example to demonstrate this persistent divergence between supply and demand. According to a local study (Ren, 1987), the graduates of political science and law from both the traditional and nontraditional institutions in the province between 1984 and 1990 could only provide 24 percent of the talent needed, and the graduates of finance and economics a little over 50 percent. Given the fact that the province was comparatively developed and had an above-average number of institutions of higher learning, the dilemma which the whole of China faced was certainly no less serious.

This disproportion in curricular structure and the resultant incongruity between supply and demand were also evident within major fields of study. Among the aggregate engineering total in 1987, for instance, the enrollment in light and textile industries merely constituted 2.4 percent of the student population and the enrollment in grain processing and food industry comprised only 1.1 percent (MOE, 1985, p. 67). With much effort, the enrollment in these two fields of study increased, respectively, to 3.3 and 2.4 percent in 1986 (Hao and Zhang, 1987, p. 18). The growth, though notable, was still far from sufficient for China, which had about 75 percent of the population working on the land and more than one billion people to clothe and feed.

The discussion of the correction of the imbalance made it clear that though great efforts and achievements had been made, significant problems remained unresolved. And considering the limited faculty resources and inadequate facilities at most colleges and universities, no fundamental solution to these long-standing problems of disproportion appeared feasible or practicable in the immediate future. What could be expected was only a long, gradual process of government policy readjustment, institutional effort and, perhaps more importantly, an increasing degree of market regulation in the drastically changed and changing political and economic context. Any rash attempt would not only contribute little to the solution of the problem, but also prove counterproductive, as borne out by the lessons of the Great Leap Forward in the late 1950s.

Solutions to Overspecialization

Parallel to the unevenness in the curricular structure, overspecialization presented another problem, reducing the capacity of Chinese higher education to meet the nation's social and economic needs. As was discussed in the historical overview, overspecialization was a legacy of the Soviet model transplanted to China during the early 1950s. The students were directly admitted to a specialization with limited, compulsory subjects for the whole of four or five years. After graduation, they were likewise assigned to work in a narrow field with a specifically defined scope of responsibility. The defects of this system were not evident when the nation's economy had been in the main centrally planned. But they became more manifest with the ongoing nationwide political and economic reforms since the late 1970s, which had brought about local initiative, enterprise autonomy and a certain degree of market regulation.

This overspecialization and its aftereffects can be exemplified by the curriculum format for the English major, which consisted mainly of a few courses designed for the acquisition of the English language skills: listening, speaking, reading, writing and translating. There were few, if any, other courses, such as offerings in literature or linguistics. Very few humanities and social science courses were offered at institutions specializing in foreign languages. Even at comprehensive universities where a wider range of courses was available, the access across disciplines was limited. As a rule, the curriculum at Chinese institutions of higher learning was so departmentalized that clear boundaries were defined and imposed. No students were allowed to take courses outside their major and their department (Wang, 1989).

Owing to this one-dimensional character of the curriculum, graduates with English majors were often deficient in breadth of knowledge. After four years of study, they might acquire an excellent command of the English language, but they were lacking in professional or specialized knowledge or expertise. Because of the deficiency, these graduates needed two or three years to adapt fully to the demands of their professional duties (Chen, 1985). Also because of the deficiency, some of the graduates were even assigned to positions incommensurate with their training.

Table 3.1

**Number of Chinese Institutions of Higher Learning
by Field of Study (1978-88)**

	1978	1979	1980	1981	1982	1983	1984	1985	1986	1987	1988
Comprehensive	32	33	32	32	32	36	38	43	46	47	49
Engineering	184	191	203	207	206	215	232	262	262	273	281
Agriculture	48	52	56	55	56	56	57	61	61	60	59
Forestry	8	9	10	10	10	11	11	11	11	11	11
Medicine & pharmacology	100	107	109	112	112	111	114	116	118	119	119
Teacher training	157	161	172	186	194	210	242	253	257	260	262
Languages	10	10	10	10	10	10	11	11	15	14	14
Finance & economics	21	22	30	36	36	44	49	62	69	74	80
Political science & law	2	6	7	7	9	10	15	24	26	25	25
Physical education	8	11	11	12	13	13	14	16	16	16	16
Arts	19	22	26	27	27	27	27	29	29	30	30
Other	9	9	9	10	10	62	92	128	134	134	129
TOTAL	598	633	675	704	715	805	902	1016	1054	1063	1075

Sources: Ministry of Education (MOE), 1985. *Achievement of Education in China.* Beijing: People's Education Press, p. 51.
State Education Commission (SEC). (1986). *Achievement of Education in China.* Beijing: People's Education Press. p. 20.
Cai, Keyong, & Zhao, Wei. (1987). Dui woguo gaojiao cunci jiegoude tansuo [Explorations of our country's higher education structure by level]. In Hao Keming & Wang Yongquan, eds. *Zhongguo Gaodeng Jiaoyu Jiegou Yanjiu [Studies in the Curricular Structure of Chinese Higher Education].* Beijing: People's Education Press.
State Education Commission (SEC), 1989. *Education in China* (1978-1988). Beijing: State Education Commission, p. 73

The same was true of graduates of other disciplines. As a consequence of their limited exposure to the knowledge and skills outside their specialization, the graduates often felt inadequate to contribute to the nation's social and economic development. The narrow curricula did not provide them with the intellectual and technical flexibility needed for the broader skills of the larger world. What happened as a result was that, on the one hand, college-trained and educated manpower was urgently needed; on the other hand,

Table 3.2

**Type of Specializations by Field of Study at
Chinese Colleges and Universities (1978-88)**

	1978	1979	1980	1981	1982	1983	1984	1985	1986	1987	1988
Engineering	396	453	537	382	366	389	362	368	367	372	378
Agriculture	49	53	60	49	46	50	51	53	53	53	53
Forestry	16	22	22	16	16	16	14	16	16	16	17
Medicine & pharmacology	47	22	29	23	22	24	22	22	25	24	25
Teacher training	41	32	40	41	40	43	43	46	43	44	47
Humanities	35	55	60	53	54	59	58	62	6	5 9	75
Natural sciences	126	149	158	153	139	146	124	125	129	133	129
Finance & economics	44	44	54	37	37	43	42	45	43	45	48
Political science & law	3	6	8	7	7	10	10	11	11	12	16
Physical education	7	8	8	9	9	12	11	12	12	14	14
Arts	55	51	63	62	58	63	60	63	62	68	68
TOTAL	**819**	**895**	**1039**	**832**	**794**	**855**	**797**	**823**	**826**	**850**	**870**

Sources: Ministry of Education (MOE), 1985. *Achievement of Education in China.*
Beijing: People's Education Press, p. 53.
State Education Commission (SEC). (1986). *Achievement of Education in China.*
Beijing: State Education Commission, p. 21.
Cai, Keyong, & Zhao, Wei. (1987). Dui woguo gaojiao cunci jiegoude tansuo [Explor-
ations of our country's higher education structure by level]. In Hao Keming & Wang
Yongquan, eds. *Zhongguo Gaodeng Jiaoyu Jiegou Yanjiu [Studies in the Curricular
Structure of Chinese Higher Education].* Beijing: People's Education Press.
Yang, Xun. (1990). Personal correspondence.

these highly trained people were often ill-suited to the job requirement. In
many cases, college graduates were assigned to positions bearing little
relevance to their highly specialized training, or they had to spend a considerable amount of time being retrained for their jobs. For instance, about
10,000 graduates from various types of automation specialization in 1982
found themselves less than useless, largely due to the overspecialized training they had received. A survey of college graduates working in 170
government departments or enterprises in 1982 revealed that 12.3 percent of
them were working in fields ill-matched with their training. Some had to do
menial jobs which did not require college education at all (Hao and Zhang,
p. 19). While this misuse and waste of talent might not be too great a problem

Table 3.3

Percentage of Enrollment by Field of Study at Chinese Colleges and Universities (1978-88)

	1978	1979	1980	1981	1982	1983	1984	1985	1986	1987	1988
Engineering	33.6	33.9	33.5	36	34.3	34.7	34.5	34.1	34.3	41.2	41.6
Agriculture	6.3	5.7	6.2	6.2	5.7	5.7	5.6	5.2	4.96	5.2	4.8
Forestry	0.9	1.1	1.0	1.1	1.0	1.1	1.1	1.0	1.02	1.2	1.1
Medicine & pharmacology	13.2	12.5	12.2	12.4	14.3	11.6	10.3	9.2	9.06	9.4	9.2
Teacher training	29.5	30.5	29.6	25.1	25.4	26.0	25.9	25.0	25.6	17.4	17.3
Humanities	5.4	5.6	5.1	5.4	5.1	5.6	6.4	7.4	6.8	6	6
Natural sciences	7.5	6.9	7.3	7.8	7.0	6.6	6.2	5.7	5.43	7.6	7.1
Finance & economics	2.1	2.1	3.3	3.7	4.7	5.9	6.9	8.7	9.01	8.2	9
Political science & law	0.2	0.3	0.5	0.8	1.2	1.5	1.8	2.1	2.3	2.2	2.3
Physical education	1.0	0.9	0.8	0.9	0.8	0.8	0.8	0.8	0.76	0.84	0.84
Arts	0.6	0.5	0.5	0.6	0.5	0.5	0.5	0.7	0.7	0.75	0.75

Sources: Ministry of Education (MOE), 1985. *Achievement of Education in China.* Beijing: People's Education Press, p. 62.
State Education Commission (SEC), 1986. *Achievement of Education in China.* Beijing: State Education Commission, p. 22.
Cai, Keyong, & Zhao, Wei. (1987). Dui woguo gaojiao cunci jiegoude tansuo [Explorations of our country's higher education structure by level]. In Hao Keming & Wang Yongquan, eds. *Zhongguo Gaodeng Jiaoyu Jiegou Yanjiu [Studies in the Curricular Structure of Chinese Higher Education].* Beijing: People's Education Press.
Yang, Xun. (1990). Personal correspondence.

in developed countries, it was devastating in China, which was a developing country with only two people out of 10,000 educated at the college level.

Fully realizing the gravity of this waste of effort and talent, institutions of higher learning began to take measures to address the problem of over-specialization in a variety of ways. One strategy, crisscrossing, created new courses at the intersection of two or more old disciplines. Another strategy was cross-fertilzation, which is a more interdisciplinary approach, produced new programs through combining natural and social sciences. A typical product of these modes of innovation was China's first School of Museum Sciences, which specialized in the excavation, research, preservation and exhibition of historical artifacts. By fully utilizing the expertise of the faculties of history, archaeology and chemistry, Northwest University established the school at its location in Xi'an, which had an abundance of historical relics buried underground (Zhang, 1989).

Another example of these curricular expansion strategies was found at Beijing University, where 400 courses in "marginal, interdisciplinary, and newly emergent disciplines that border on the applied humanities and the natural sciences" were initiated by the nine humanities departments of the university (Yao, 1985). Keenly aware that science and technology in the contemporary era are advancing at an unprecedented rate, the faculties of these departments joined forces and, through interpenetration and cross-fertilization, made this impressive number of elective courses available to the students with a view to letting them "receive more multi-faceted and broader knowledge" (Yao). The effort of the faculty was highly appreciated by the students, who competed for places in these elective classes. In some classrooms, even the floor was taken up completely by the students (Yao).

Similar efforts to expand course offerings were made by other institutions of higher learning. The South China Teachers University, for example, increased its elective courses at the rate of 50 a year during the early 1980s. By 1985, the number of elective courses offered at the university had increased to 230, which made up 20 percent of the total class hours (Li, 1985).

With the expansion of the course offerings at these and hundreds of other colleges and universities, the curriculum for Chinese higher education had undergone a significant change. From the former one-dimensional, compulsory courses, there emerged, in the 1980s, a plural or multidimensional curricular structure. The general pattern of this structure was three-pronged: core curricula, distribution requirements and free electives. Included in the core curricula were those courses essential for a student's major field of study as well as subjects in political education, physical culture, practical training, productive labor, and military training. The distribution requirements encompassed courses in the students' specialization, in political theory and education and in social or natural sciences. The free electives usually covered the fields outside the students' major fields of study. All categories of courses, required or elective, had increased in number, but it was in the elective course offerings that a greater expansion had been made. And, predictably, it was at the comprehensive universities, where faculty expertise was relatively diversified, that the increase had been more marked.

Besides the expansion in course offerings, other measures were adopted to remedy the problem of overspecialization. For instance, with the introduction of double major and major/minor, students who had high grades were allowed and encouraged to choose and work for a second major or a minor during their junior or senior years. In addition to this practice, a more drastic innovation was initiated. The Beijing Agricultural University, for example, discarded the conventional nationwide practice of enrolling students directly into a specialization and asked the applicants to indicate their preference for a department instead. When enrolled, all the students were required during the first three semesters to take the general foundation courses. Following this stage, the students would spend two more semesters taking the interdepartmental core courses for agricultural sciences. Only after this broad study would the students be asked to choose and finalize their major in accordance with social needs and their personal aptitudes and interests. They were requested to complete their majors during the remaining three semesters (*Guangming Daily*, August 1, 1988, p. 2).

Responding to Social Needs—Further Expansion
of the Curriculum

Obviously, the measures that had been taken to resolve the problem of overspecialization significantly broadened the curriculum. After years of being subjected to a narrow scope of required courses, the students were being provided with a vast array of courses, both required and elective. Colleges and universities broke down the often impermeable walls between academic departments and disciplines to permit and encourage insights from one academic field to cross-fertilize with those from others. In an age of rapid technological change and tremendous growth of scientific information, such joint efforts were seen to be essential for the advancement of knowledge and skills.

In addition to enlarging the scope of their course offerings, colleges and universities responded to the larger world. Institutions of higher learning began to dismantle not only the walls between academic departments on their own campuses, but also the walls between themselves and the outside world. Instead of confining themselves to their ivory towers, institutions of higher learning began to look out from their vantage point, respond to the needs of society and render services they were in a unique position to provide.

In fact, Chinese colleges and universities since modern times had not been ivory towers. The extensive restructuring in the early 1950s was specifically aimed at a more effective and direct contribution on the part of the institutions of higher learning to the national effort for economic rehabilitation. The guideline from the late 1950s to the late 1970s that "education must serve proletarian politics and be combined with productive labour" (CCP, 1958) consolidated the link between schools and the society. In particular, the 300-some institutions sponsored and administered by central government ministries were meant to serve specific needs of the nation's economic development. With the new guideline since the late 1970s that "education must serve socialist construction" (CCP, 1985), the link between institutions of higher learning and society had naturally grown even stronger. And since the late 1970s this link had become multidimensional as well. In addition to maintaining the previously vertical relationship with mandatory teaching and research assignments from the line of authority, institutions of higher learning took advantage of their newly gained autonomies and began to establish heterogeneous, horizontal links on the basis of equality and mutual benefit. As a result, huge numbers of teaching-research-production conglomerates were established both among universities and between universities and government departments and enterprises (SEC, 1989, p, 76).

An example of the interinstitutional collaboration was the Nanjing-Johns Hopkins Center for Chinese and American Studies. Jointly run by Nanjing University of China and Johns Hopkins University of the United States and opened in the fall of 1986, the center offered a two-semester, graduate-level curriculum in culture, economics, politics, foreign policy, international relations and law, modern history and U.S.-China relations. The American students, who made up half of the total student body, mainly focused their studies on China in the Chinese language, while the Chinese students, who made up the other half, concentrated on the study of the United States and the West in English. The purpose of this joint venture was to train professional people in Sino-American affairs and teachers/researchers in the field of Sino-American relations (Nanjing-Johns Hopkins Center, 1989).

Interinstitutional cooperation was also conducted in other forms: joint training of Ph.D. students and managerial personnel, opening of laboratories and exchange of information, material and faculty members (Zhang, 1988). Even more extensive than the various forms of interinstitutional cooperation were the tripartite teaching-research-production combines established between colleges and universities and government departments and enterprises. Qinghua University, for instance, capitalized on its concentration of skilled personnel, technical strengths, knowledge and information and conducted joint research projects and scientific and technological exchanges with virtually all provinces, autonomous regions and municipalities of China. It also formed 13 scientific and production associations with factories and provided technological consultation and training for numerous enterprises. These aggressive endeavors, in turn, gave rise to a host of custom-made courses in interdisciplinary and frontier fields of study (Liu, 1985).

As the foremost polytechnical university in China, Qinghua was, of course, well equipped in terms of both human and material resources to undertake projects on such a grand scale. But many lesser universities likewise pursued similar joint programs to the best of their ability and substantially expanded their curricular offerings. The Northwest College of Light Industry, for instance, had formed since 1984 teaching/research/production conglomerates with as many as 70 institutions, enterprises and government departments. What emerged from these collaborative programs was a host of disciplines and courses such as hide processing, leather production, food engineering, packaging and enamelware manufacturing, as well as the educational focuses of curriculum content renewal and teaching material development (Pan, 1987). Similarly, the Jiangsu Agricultural College collaborated with the Central Land Reclamation Bureau and added to their curriculum many new disciplines such as farm produce processing and storage. With a different focus, the Yangzhou Teachers College broadened its curriculum to include commercial economics and commercial accountancy by joining forces with the Ministry of Commerce (Ye, 1987).

Signs of Curriculum Transformation

The expansion of the curriculum resulting from the efforts to overcome the negative effects of overspecialization and to respond to social and economic needs not only broke the unitary mode of limited, compulsory curriculum, but also brought about the internal transformation of China's institutions of higher learning in terms of curriculum development. For example, the former Shanghai Institute of Foreign Languages, which had a curriculum only for foreign language studies, was becoming a liberal arts institution with foreign languages as the major medium of instruction. Besides the former courses aimed at the acquisition of language skills, the institution began to offer such courses as economics, history, law, religion, sociology, journalism, psychology, international news media, foreign trade, international economic law, foreign affairs management and computer science. The students were required to concentrate on one liberal arts field and to study one or two foreign languages. Appropriately, the institute was renamed the Shanghai International Studies University (Shen, 1989 and *CEN*, 1985, *13* (2), 38-39).

A similar transformation occurred at the former Foreign Languages Institute of Beijing, the foremost institution of its kind in China with 29 languages taught. Upgraded to Beijing Foreign Studies University, it had likewise substantially expanded its curriculum and broadened its program requirement. The English Department, for example, began to offer courses in journalism, international communication, foreign culture and Western civilization to augment its traditional courses in language skills, linguistics and literature (Wu, 1986). Evidently, the university was expanding beyond its former, one-dimensional course offering and becoming a liberal arts college, as was the case with its counterpart in Shanghai (*CEN*, 1985, *13* (2), 39).

This internal transformation occurred more rapidly at comprehensive universities, which had more diversified faculty expertise and hence more potential for course expansion. Part of this expansion consisted of reversing the narrow specialization that resulted from the nationwide restructuring in the early 1950s. The comprehensive universities, which had had actually only science and liberal arts courses, began to move back toward a true comprehensiveness. Fudan University, which had been stripped of its commerce and engineering in the early 1950s, established the School of Technological Sciences to coordinate the teaching and research in computer science, electrical engineering, material science and applied mechanics (Rubin, 1983). Nanjing University established a medical school and a school of international commerce (Qu, 1988). Conversely, Qinghua University, which had had its liberal arts moved out following the emulation of the Soviet model, reintroduced courses in sciences and humanities (Zhou, 1989).

The same trend could be perceived at lower-echelon institutions as well. Zhejiang University, which had specialized in engineering, was becoming a university with a combination of engineering, sciences, liberal arts and management while maintaining engineering as the core in the curriculum (Lu, 1989). Northwest University, which was administered by the provincial authority, began to become a multidisciplined institution with 46 types of specializations in not only arts and sciences, but also law, management, and engineering (Zhang, 1989).

Open-Door Policy and Curriculum Expansion

The trend toward a wider, more comprehensive curriculum which had been made possible by the broadening of course offerings was, viewed from a wider perspective, attributable to China's pursuance of the open-door policy. The policy secured for Chinese institutions of higher learning two sources of rare but significant intellectual manpower: an increasing number of foreign scholars employed to teach at Chinese universities and thousands of

Chinese who had returned from overseas with their newly acquired knowledge and skills.

Since the late 1970s, over 10,000 scholars from about 30 countries had been invited to teach at Chinese colleges and universities (SEC, 1989, p. 93). Whether on a long-term or a short-term basis, these scholars brought with them expertise in the discipline areas in which China had been weak. A case in point was the interdisciplinary program of American studies. According to the 1984 report by an American delegation across the fields of American history, literature, politics and culture, China needed much enrichment to establish an equivalent of an American concept of American studies as an interdisciplinary course. At the suggestion of the delegation, American professors in relevant disciplines were subsequently sent as Fulbright scholars by the U.S. government or invited as guest lecturers by Chinese institutions to initiate or reinforce studies in this field (*CEN*, 1985, *13* (3), 16).

Another component of this "loaned" talent came from extensive institutional exchanges with the support and endorsement of the State Education Commission. Since 1978, over 200 Chinese colleges and universities had established sister relations with about 400 institutions of higher learning in more than 40 countries and regions (SEC, p. 94). These relationships resulted in the exchange of personnel, cooperation in research, exchange of books and materials and convening of symposia, contributing significantly to course offerings at Chinese colleges and universities.

More vital than this first component of intellectual power, which was expensive and transient, were the thousands of Chinese students and scholars who had returned to China upon completing their advanced studies and research in an increasing number of industrialized countries. During the decade of 1978-1988, over 80,000 Chinese scholars were sent to over 70 countries of the world. Of these, 22,000 completed their studies or training and returned (He, 1989). With new knowledge and skills, these returned scholars began to play a significant part in enlarging the course offerings at Chinese institutions of higher learning. In 1987, 328 of Qinghua University's professors who had returned from their studies overseas offered 385 new courses for both undergraduate and graduate students (Zhang, 1988). In fact, most of the new courses in frontier and interdisciplinary areas newly designed and offered at most Chinese institutions of higher learning were either taken up or taken over from foreign professors by returned scholars (Bai, 1989).

Improving Instructional Methods

"Whatever the form of curriculum revision, a large measure of its success was going to depend on molding methods of instruction by the same spirit governing the curriculum revision." These words, by Brubacher and Rudy (1976, p. 280) in their documentary history of American higher education, also hold true for Chinese institutions of higher learning. To maximize the effect of the more rational, diversified and flexible curricula that had been gradually developed through painstaking efforts, it was imperative for Chinese educators to reform their outdated and often stifling teaching methods (Wang, 1989). Characterized by spoon-feeding and memorization since ancient times, these methods deprived the students of their creativity and initiative. With these old-fashioned instructional methods, the students were "programmed to sit in large lecture halls, assiduously take notes, and memorize what the teacher has told them without ever having the opportunity for class discussion or analysis of material" (Rubin, 1983).

This passivity in the classroom was best exemplified by a personal account of an American professor who had taught law in China. The professor began his first class with a question, but nobody volunteered to answer. Having been warned of the reticence of Chinese students in class, he turned to his alternate plan by calling on a student. The question was repeated several times, but still "not a sound passed from his lips." Then a long silence ensued:

> I had the better brace and the teacher's mantle of authority; he had thousands of years of tradition and home field. Our determination was equal...The scale teetered for what seemed an eternity; he in silence, me taking occasional sips [of tea] punctuated with asides from my interpreter, "This is not going to work, the students would prefer you lecture." [Kanter, 1985]

This was, of course, an extreme case, but there is no denying that Chinese students were conditioned to be passively instructed by the teachers, who in turn were equally accustomed to giving straight lectures without making efforts to elicit questions and to organize discussions. In class, the students listened to the teacher and took copious notes; after class, they went over their notes and tried to memorize everything that had been said in class and written down in their notebooks. The assignments and examinations were likewise confined to what had been done in class. And because of inadequate facilities and limited library holdings, laboratory hours were few, and outside reading infrequent. As a result, Chinese students were good at absorbing new information and knowledge, but limited in their horizon and deficient in analyzing and synthesizing what they had learned. Although scoring high grades, they often lacked ability and skills to solve practical problems. Both methodological and administrative measures were taken to resolve these problems in the 1980s. Updated, more effective methods such as elicitation, discussions and seminars were combined with modern technologies in the form of audiovisual aids and computers to invigorate and improve classroom instruction. Administratively, class hours were reduced, independent study was introduced, a credit system was instituted and examinations were reformed. While the improvement of methods and the use of modern technologies as a whole had been advocated for decades, some measures, both administrative and instructional, that had been adopted were comparatively new, innovative and drastic. The innovations can be best illustrated by the experiments at the following two universities, one a medical institution and the other a leading polytechnic.

The Zhongshan Medical University

The Zhongshan Medical University carried out three experiments with teaching and examination. The first experiment, which adopted independent study as the main form of learning, was conducted as a reaction to the domination of the outdated, conservative and stifling classroom instructional methods of the past. In the first semester of the 1983-1984 academic year, the university randomly divided the 212 freshmen into two groups of equal number. While the first group was taught by conventional methods, a series of experiments was undertaken with the second. Class hours were cut by 50 percent. The textbooks were few and highly selected, but the outside reading lists were lengthened. Laboratory work was made more investigative and exploratory in nature. And the time spent on clinical practice was considerably increased. After four years, the two groups were contrasted through comprehensive tests. While no clear difference was evident between the two groups in terms of their study of required, basic courses, the experimental group demonstrated a much greater ability in synthesizing information, solving problems, analyzing cases and dealing with emergency situations.

The second experiment at the Zhongshan Medical University was the use of English as the medium of instruction. For nine consecutive years, students with a good command of English had been selected and put in special classes where the core medical courses were conducted in English. Statistics showed that the graduates from these classes were not only excellent in these medical courses, but also outstanding in their overall command of the English language. Both the participating teachers and the students had benefitted.

The third experiment at the Zhongshan Medical University concerned the nature of examinations. At most Chinese colleges and universities, examination questions for a course of study were, as a rule, written by the professors who taught the course. Likewise, the examination papers were evaluated by the professors who had written the questions. It followed that the grades were often a reflection of the viewpoints of the professors rather than an accurate indication of the real learning and ability of the students.

So along with their experiment introducing independent study as the principal form of learning, the Zhongshan Medical University began in 1986 to entrust committees with the composing, screening and reviewing of the examination questions and the evaluation of examination papers. Furthermore, three measures were taken to ensure the quality of questions. First, the questions were diversified to include those meant to test the students' comprehension and application as well as retention. Second, scientific measurements were applied to gauge the validity, difficulty and reliability of the questions. Third, steps were taken to avoid the repetition of questions within three years. With the introduction of these measures, the students' grades became lower for a time, but teaching and learning were put on a more solid basis (*Guangming Daily,* October, 9, 1989, p. 1).

The Xi'an Jiaotong University

Following the principle of teaching according to the aptitude and ability of the students, the Xi'an Jiaotong University began, in 1984, to employ a variety of methods to train students who were classified into five categories according to their performance and abilities.

1) Through comprehensive examinations at the conclusion of the first year, outstanding students were selected to enter honors programs with special, custom-made courses. These students often completed their programs ahead of schedule. They were then given the option to pursue graduate studies without being required to take graduate enrollment examinations or to work for a second undergraduate degree in another discipline with 25 percent of the required credit hours of the discipline.

2) Students who had excellent grades during the whole of the four undergraduate years were permitted to pursue graduate studies with an exemption from graduate enrollment examinations.

3) Students who had completed their undergraduate courses with 360 to 370 credit hours received normal BA degrees.

4) Students who had failed to complete the prescribed number of credit hours during the first two years of their undergraduate studies were assigned for a period of one academic year to courses which would be designed for their specific needs. When they reached the 270 to 280 credit hour requirement at the end of the third year, they were graduated as short-cycle course students without a BA.

5) Students who did not complete 50 percent of the required credit hours during the first year were disqualified and made to leave the university.

The rationale for these different approaches used with different categories of students, according to the university authorities, was to break the "Iron Rice Bowl" so that the students would apply themselves in their studies. Among the 1987 class, the outstanding students of the first category made up 2.4 percent of the total enrollment, the excellent students of the second category 20 percent, the poor students of the fourth category 2 percent, and the very poor students of the last category 1 percent. The rest were classified as good students who made up about 69 percent. (Zhang and Zhu, 1987).

Summary

Before the late 1970s, the curriculum of Chinese higher education was narrow and unbalanced. It consisted of a single category of required courses concentrating on a highly specialized field of study. The students were enrolled directly into a specialization and exposed to a limited number of required courses during the whole period of their undergraduate studies.

The imbalance of the curriculum was reflected in the comparatively rapid development of engineering at the expense of such liberal arts and professional disciplines as political science, law, finance and economics. These deficiencies in the curriculum did not fully manifest themselves and become adequately recognized until China began to engage in extensive political and economic reforms since the late 1970s.

Great efforts had been made since the late 1970s to correct the imbalance. By means of government policy readjustment, institutional initiative and market regulation, the neglected fields of study began to register substantial growth. Though there was still a gap between the demand and supply in these fields of study, the grave disproportion had at least begun to be corrected.

Equally notable progress had been made in broadening the curriculum. From a unitary required-course format, the institutions of higher learning began to move toward a diversified, flexible and responsive curriculum consisting of core courses, required distribution, and a considerable number of free electives. The expansion of the curriculum had been made possible by both intra- and interinstitutional efforts. The programs of cooperative teaching, research and production established between institutions of higher learning on the one hand and government departments and enterprises on the other further promoted curriculum development. By designing new programs to better respond to social needs, colleges and universities not only revitalized their teaching and research, but also began to change their orientation from a former state of narrow specialization. Some language institutions, for instance, were becoming colleges of liberal arts. Comprehensive universities, which had only a curriculum in sciences and liberal arts, began to move toward true comprehensiveness by developing disciplines in engineering and other fields. By the same token, major polytechnical universities began to add social sciences and humanities to their curriculum.

The expansion and the transformation of the curriculum were attributable to China's pursuance of the open-door policy, which had brought into China many scholars from overseas and enabled thousands of Chinese scholars to learn advanced sciences and technologies in industrialized countries. Without these components of much-needed intellectual power, the expansion of the curriculum would certainly not have been so dramatic, and the transformation of the curriculum would not have been possible.

In addition to the tremendous expansion of the curriculum, teaching methods, which were predominately spoon-feeding and memorization, were being improved through a variety of means: The use of new approaches and technologies, the reduction of class hours, the introduction of the credit-hour system and the emphasis on independent study and practical training.

4

Faculty

"**R**arely can improvement in education occur without the active cooperation of the faculty" (Bok, 1982, p. 184). But little cooperation can be expected from the faculty unless there is a favorable environment with congenial policies and attractive career prospects. Unfortunately, such an environment did not exist in China before the decade of reform and openness.

Like other intellectuals, university professors were distrusted and, therefore, subjected to protracted thought reforms through participation in frequent political campaigns and integration with worker-peasant masses. This discrimination grew into radical action during the Cultural Revolution. In addition to being distrusted, university professors were labeled as "bourgeois intellectuals," accused of sabotaging China's educational cause and made to reform themselves through hard labor either on campus or in remote rural areas. Many were physically abused and then deprived of their basic human rights. Professionally, academic promotion was suspended, and teaching and research were interrupted. When the Cultural Revolution ended, Chinese colleges and universities were left with a faculty not only ill-prepared and insufficient, but also psychologically traumatized.

Multiple measures were taken to remedy this situation in the markedly changed political and economic climate. First, the false charges and injustices leveled at university professors were redressed, and the contributions of the university professors to the building of the nation were recognized. With the stigma removed and the social status recognized, a greater degree of freedom in academic pursuits was made possible. Secondly, a variety of strategies were employed for professional development.

The Recognition of Contribution

During the 17 years prior to the Cultural Revolution, university professors and other intellectuals in China were utilized as well as feared. According to rhetoric, they were precious human assets deserving respect and trust. But in fact, the attitude toward them had been, from the early days of the Communist revolution, ambivalent. On the one hand, the knowledge and expertise of the intellectuals were urgently needed; on the other, the influence of the often nonconformist thinking of the intellectuals was regarded as a potential threat. So during the years between 1949 and 1966, the intellectuals were "united, educated, and remolded" (CIER, 1983, p. 304). They were made to participate in a succession of political campaigns to cleanse their thinking and conform to the orthodoxy of Marxism-Leninism-Mao Zedong thought. Violations of the intellectuals' basic rights and freedoms were frequent; divergent views were often suppressed and punished. Periodically, some degree of tolerance would be granted, and differing views would be invited, but policy fluctuations were frequent and violent. Though they were declared to be mental workers who had no conflicting interests with the leading proletariat, the intellectuals could not be certain what would happen to them in case the CCP policy emphasis shifted (CIER, p. 304).

And indeed, what befell them soon after all the excruciating thought reforms was more severe than they had predicted. During the Cultural Revolution, the intellectuals were classified as the "stinking ninth category" of class enemies, coming after the eight other categories: landlords, rich peasants, counterrevolutionaries, bad elements, anti-CCP rightists, renegades, enemy agents and capitalist roaders, all of whom were seen as detrimental to the CCP interest and subjected to the proletarian dictatorship.

Then, as the Cultural Revolution progressed, years of accusation, confession, persecution and exile followed. Many professors managed to survive this nightmare with lingering psychological trauma. Some died before the wrongs could be redressed. These injustices were evidenced by numerous official documents. A special report about the persecution of university faculty by the former Shaanxi Provincial Bureau of Higher Education revealed, for example, that 53.6 percent of the 3838 faculty members of the institutions of higher learning in 1969 had their cases put on file for investigation and prosecution (*China Education Yearbook: 1949-1984, Local Education*, 1986, p. 1176). Another report from Gansu Province disclosed that 72 professors and educational leaders of six colleges and universities in the province died following the insufferable humiliations inflicted on them. (*Yearbook*, 1986, p. 1221).

Fortunately, the discrimination against and the persecution of the intellectuals were finally brought to an end. When the Gang of Four, the chief culprits responsible for the crimes, was brought to justice, and the emphasis of the nation was shifted from mass class struggle to extensive economic development, conditions for the intellectual community took a slow but sharp turn for the better. And the due recognition of the intellectuals' social status and vital contribution was championed. In his keynote speech at the National Science Conference in 1978, Deng Xiaoping asserted that the intellectuals were scientific and technical components of the working class worthy of full recognition and trust (1984, p. 108). At the subsequent National Education Conference held in the same year, Deng again adamantly claimed that those who worked with their minds were also members of the proletariat and emphasized that teachers were the key to the training of large numbers of personnel indispensable to the nation's economic development and, therefore, must no longer suffer any discrimination (p. 125).

Deng's pleas on behalf of the intellectuals were widely publicized and supported. Consistent with his speeches and with the drastic change in the nation's political life, task forces were organized at different levels to correct the false accusations and injustices inflicted on the intellectuals. Educational departments and universities in Gansu Province, for example, had reversed by 1986 the wrong accusations leveled at 1447 of the 1450 professors of the province. The 72 who had died were posthumously rehabilitated (p. 1226). As the wrongs were redressed, the confiscated property was returned, the stopped or docked salaries were recompensed, personal dossiers were cleared up and the families were reunited. In the wake of the rehabilitation, university professors were restored to their former positions of teaching and research. Many were appointed to leading positions as chairmen of academic departments, directors of research institutes and presidents or vice presidents of colleges and universities. Though there were minor policy fluctuations during subsequent years, university professors had obtained relative freedom in academic pursuit and some power in university management had been secured. The contribution of the intellectuals to the nation's modernization endeavors had begun to be duly recognized. As observed by an American scholar, "[Chinese] intellectuals as a social group have regained some political influence, professional autonomy, and social status" (Hamrin, 1987).

The recognition was formalized by the designation of September 10 as National Teachers' Day by the National People's Congress at its meeting in January 1985. The occasion was marked with a variety of activities that aimed at promoting respect for teachers and for knowledge and at commending outstanding teachers. All these activities constituted part of the continuing effort to raise the social status of teachers and to call nationwide attention to the importance of education.

The Restoration of Academic Promotion

Following the redressing of false charges against university professors and the restoration of their former positions of teaching and research came the reinstatement of academic promotion, which had been suspended since the mid-1960s. Because of the hiatus, the senior-rank faculty of full and associate professors were few in number and old in age. Many highly promising, competent young and middle-aged faculty members had not been advanced to the senior academic rank and correspondingly remunerated. Of the 206,000 full-time faculty members working at Chinese institutions of higher learning in 1978, only 2300 were professors and 3500 were associate professors, representing respectively 1.3 and 2.7 percent of the total (MOE, 1985, p. 112-113). Even when promotion was resumed in the late 1970s, not much improvement was made. In 1984, for example, the percentage of full and associate professors combined only made up about 10 percent of the total (SEC, 1986, p. 38). By way of comparison, over 50 percent of the university faculty in 1947 had full or associate professor titles (MOE, p. 103). More uneven and serious than the low percentage of high-ranking faculty were the disproportionate age distribution and the problem of aging among the faculty with senior rank. It was reported that during the academic year of 1984-1985, there were only four professors in the entire country who were between 40 and 45 years of age, making up less than 0.1 percent of the total. In contrast, over 40 percent of the full professors were over 71 years old. Among the associate professors, only 0.3 percent were under the age of 40, while 20 percent were over the age of 60 (Huang, 1985).

These problems and the overwhelming backlog of work made the restoration of academic promotion a formidable task. After years of study and pilot and field tests, the restoration was fully unfolded, and notable progress was made. By 1988, 15,000 full and 75,000 associate professors were finally appointed. As a result of the appointment, the average age of full professors dropped from 69 to 59 and that of the associate professors from 56 to 53. More significantly, outstanding people in their thirties and twenties were promoted to the rank of full or associate professor on the basis of merit (*Guangming Daily,* January 30, 1988, p. 3). By this time university faculty members with the title of full and associate professors accounted for approximately 24 percent of the total.

Some distinguishing features of the rank-advancement effort should be identified. First, the lifetime retention of an academic title began to be abolished. Second, a quota worked out on the basis of an optimal teacher-student ratio was imposed. Third, a process of assessment and appointment was enforced. And fourth, a mechanism of checks and balances was introduced.

Before the 1980s, when faculty members were promoted to the senior rank, they would hold the title for the rest of their lives, whether they were productive or not. And in case of transfer, the title was still recognized and retained. The new system abandoned this practice and substituted it with a two-year appointment. Though renewal was in most cases automatic, there was still the risk of losing the rank if the promoted faculty member proved unfit for reappointment or was out of service for an extended period of time. In cases of transfer, the title would no longer be valid. Moreover, compulsory retirement was enforced for both full and associate male professors at the age of 60, and female professors at the age of 55. Upon retirement, the academic titles would be removed, and the academic positions would be vacated for the appointment of others.

Closely linked with compulsory retirement was the ratio between teacher and student. To ensure efficiency and minimize waste of the precious human resources, the SEC set an average teacher-student ratio at 1:8. With the ratio set and the enrollment centrally planned, the size of the faculty would be fixed (Zhang, 1989). Among this fixed size of faculty, the percentage of different ranks was likewise stipulated. Though the percentage varied from institution to institution and from one major discipline to another, faculty members holding the senior rank of professors and associate professors were not supposed to exceed an average of 25 percent (Wang, 1990). This guideline made faculty turnover essential.

Following these guidelines from the SEC, institutions of higher learning established, at both the departmental and institutional levels, academic committees which were comprised of representatives of faculty members. The mission of these committees was to review the qualifications of applicants for various academic positions and then to vote by secret ballot to short-list and select candidates for appointment by the president.

At this stage of the process of academic promotion, the mechanism of checks and balances was practiced. No academic position could be appointed until the majority of the committee members had carefully evaluated and approved the qualifications of the candidates. However, the qualifications did not automatically lead to appointment. The ultimate decision for appointment rested with the president, who must consider the university's needs for teaching and research and abide by the quota which had been established and imposed by the SEC or provincial-level commissions for education.

The limitation of the quota caused two major problems: the uncertain future of those who had been assessed as qualifying for a higher academic rank but were not appointed, and a surplus of faculty beyond the mandated teacher-student ratio. The average teacher-student ratio was 1:5.4 in 1987 (SEC, 1989, p. 72), significantly lower than the specified 1:8.

Solutions to these delicate problems were also twofold. Those who did not get appointed were encouraged to seek employment in newer, less well known institutions where the faculty was insufficient and, therefore, their appointment could be ensured. Thus the underused talent was redirected to institutions where it could become a valuable asset. The other solution to the problem of appointment was to accept research projects and commissioned students from the horizontal linkages between institutions and government agencies and enterprises so that the excess faculty could be absorbed.

Solutions to Inbreeding

The appointment to academic ranks was, no doubt, a precondition for enthusiastic and creative contributions expected from the university professors. But if adequate qualifications were not reached, the promotion would become meaningless and counterproductive. For the long-term development of Chinese higher education, the quality of faculty was more significant than the appointment of academic ranks.

The quality of the Chinese university faculty was largely determined by the way they were selected and recruited. Unlike American institutions of higher learning, which advertise faculty vacancies through various channels and select and recruit faculty members from a wide pool of applicants, Chinese colleges and universities filled faculty positions primarily by retaining their own graduates. This problem of inbreeding was particularly serious at prestigious, national-echelon universities, which "regard their own graduates as superior and see the retention of the best as the only way of ensuring academic quality" (Hayhoe, p. 84). The less prestigious, lower-echelon institutions, either unwilling to accept or unable to obtain the second- or third-best from other institutions, likewise kept their top graduates to serve as faculty members. Over the years this practice had thus been perpetuated. Each year the universities would submit a request specifying the number or percentage of their graduates to be retained for faculty replenishment. And with few modifications, the request would be granted.

The extent of the inbreeding was evidenced by statistics. In her 1982 research report of the reform of Chinese higher education, Pepper stated that 90 percent or even more of the teaching and administrative staff were comprised of a university's own graduates (p. 161). This percentage remained largely unchanged since the completion of Pepper's research project. Lanzhou University, which was a key, comprehensive university under the SEC, reported in 1986 that of the 439 young faculty members hired over a four-year period, 84.5 percent were homebred (*Yearbook*, p. 1227). In his speech at the Third Conference of Sino-U.S. University Presidents, Wu Zhuoqun (1988), president of Jilin University, disclosed that of the 434 MA or PhD recipients his university had recruited as faculty members between 1981 and 1987, 410 had been trained at his own university, which constituted 94.5 percent of the total number of the faculty that had been recruited during a seven-year period. The percentage might be considerably lower at new, local institutions, especially short-cycle, specialized colleges or community colleges. But one local, three-year college for teacher training stated that due to the difficulty of obtaining qualified people from the outside, they had to select and appoint about 50 percent of their new faculty members from among the college's own graduating students (Ban, 1989).

This serious problem of inbreeding was compounded by the limited mobility of the university faculty and the time-honored Chinese cultural tradition of respect for elders, particularly one's teachers. This resulted in a community of scholars who were highly similar in modes of thinking and styles of conducting teaching and research. The difference, if any, lay only in age. Academic cross-fertilization was hardly possible or existent; creativity and competition were stifled. Worse still, the stagnation often created contagious parochialism and inertia which were detrimental to a healthy, vigorous academic ethos.

These drawbacks of inbreeding had long been recognized. But due to the protracted nature of the problem, no quick, lasting solutions could be expected. Without an overhaul of the country's employment system, no fundamental cure to this problem was likely to be found. In spite of the seemingly insurmountable difficulty, however, many local, piecemeal and restricted strategies had been attempted during the ten years 1978 to 1988 to solve the problem.

One of the strategies adopted was to select students, or rather prospective faculty members, for training at other colleges and universities. The institutions that were eager to diversify their faculty, but found it hard to get graduates from other institutions, often selected, from among their juniors, candidates who were outstanding in academic achievement, promising as potential teachers and willing to accept the calling of the teaching profession. Those students were then sent to a number of other institutions for two years of undergraduate studies or even some nondegree graduate work. Upon completion of their studies, these students would return to their home institutions and take up faculty positions. This practice called for intercollegiate cooperation and often involved financial compensation to the host colleges and universities. With the autonomies that had been granted to institutions of higher learning, these technicalities were usually solved easily to mutual satisfaction. Generally, this measure was taken by newer, lower-echelon institutions and institutions in less developed interior regions of the country. And it proved to be an effective way to solve the problem of inbreeding (*Yearbook*, p. 239).

Another measure taken was to commission the training of young faculty members at institutions with strong faculty and up-to-date laboratory and library facilities. Eleven of the colleges and universities in Inner Mongolia, for example, had 1100 young faculty members trained from 1979 to 1986 in ten institutions of higher learning in Beijing and one medical university under the administration of the Ministry of Public Health. From 1978 to 1985 Qinghua University accepted and trained 1149 faculty members from colleges and universities located in many parts of the country (Lu, 1986). This type of program was normally conducted through the sister-school relationship. With the establishment of horizontal liaisons between institutions of higher learning, this strategy for overcoming the drawbacks of inbreeding had come to be widely adopted (*Yearbook*, p. 239).

Working as guest lecturers at institutions of similar caliber comprised one more measure to counter the problem of inbreeding. With mutual agreement, faculty members, especially the comparatively young, inexperienced members, were sent to each other's institutions to lecture, but at reduced workload. The remainder of their time was then spent on refresher courses, research or the observation of teaching (Huang, 1985). Under similar arrangements, many universities brought in highly experienced technical personnel to give lectures or to collaborate in research. Qinghua University made it a rule that experienced personnel from outside academia should be either invited to give occasional lectures or appointed as adjunct professors (Liang, 1988).

In addition to these remedies already in practice, some administrative measures were suggested. It was recommended that a fixed proportion of new faculty members be required to be graduates from other institutions and that this percentage be gradually increased. The second measure suggested was that institutions of higher learning should cooperate in their graduate programs and exchange graduate students. The third proposed measure encouraged the supervisors for graduate students to send their best students to work at other institutions. No graduates would be allowed to work at their alma mater unless they had served as faculty members for two to three years at another institution (Li, 1988).

Among all the options available for improving faculty at institutions of higher learning in China, the one considered most desirable was to grant faculty members the opportunity to work for advanced degrees in foreign countries, especially in the United States. Although the key, national-echelon institutions of higher learning had the most serious problem of inbreeding, they were the most capable of solving it, mainly through scholarly and academic exchanges with institutions overseas. While the faculty of many local, new colleges could scarcely dream of even a short academic trip to other countries, it was not uncommon for more than half of the faculty of most key institutions of higher learning to have a couple of years' experience overseas.

Improving Faculty Quality

In addition to the inbred faculty composition, low qualifications and dispro-portionate age distribution called for attention and solution. The 1987 statistics showed that among all the full-time university faculty in China, only 12.6 percent had had graduate training. Of these, only 0.5 percent held PhD's (Li, 1988). The problem of low qualifications was, in turn, exacer-bated by an unbalanced age distribution. Due to the explosive expansion of enrollment, full-time university faculty in 1987 almost doubled the 1978 figure (MOE, 1985, p. 102; *Beijing Review*, July 17-23, 1989, p. 26). And because the new recruits were mostly recent graduates, young people under the age of 30 constituted 35 percent of the total number of faculty members (Li, 1988). Having been students most of the time, these new faculty members had had little experience in teaching or even in life. It was, therefore, imperative that they be trained for the job.

An obvious solution to the problem of insufficient qualifications was to recruit MA and PhD recipients to replenish the faculty. While this was beginning to take place, the universities continued to address the urgent problem of upgrading the knowledge and skill of those already on the job.

So a wide variety of programs had been developed. One of them was a one-year visiting-scholar scheme coordinated by the SEC. Nationwide, 87 colleges and universities with relatively strong faculty, adequate laboratory facilities, and sufficient library holdings were designated as host institutions to accept faculty members from lesser institutions for teaching, joint research, textbook development and graduate-student supervision. Since 1986 when the program was initiated, over 500 young and comparatively inexperienced faculty members had been thus professionally trained (Shu, 1988). To coordinate this and similar programs, the SEC established two centers, one in Beijing, which was affiliated with the Beijing Normal University, the leading university of its kind in China, and the other in Wuhan, affiliated with Wuhan University, a major key comprehensive university in Central China (Huang, 1985).

Other programs for this purpose under the auspices of the SEC included in-service, intensive courses in major fields of study for young assistant teachers, summer seminars, curriculum and textbook committees and symposia. It was reported that since the late 1970s, over 40,000 university faculty members had gone through refresher classes or in-service training of one kind or another (Zhu, 1988).

More extensive and innovative than the SEC-sponsored programs were a wide variety of classes conducted at the institutional level. Nankai University in Tianjin, for example, had been organizing since 1981 intensive courses in sociology, which had been until recently politically dangerous and therefore an almost unexplored subject (Huang, 1985). With the endorsement of the SEC, classes of this type had been almost universally organized in every major field of study for young teachers. Besides these off-campus programs, in-service courses in computer technology and foreign languages were widespread.

Other innovations included the introduction of a mentor system whereby relatively young, inexperienced faculty members were regularly tutored and supervised in teaching and research (Yuan, 1988). Under this system, young faculty members were usually entrusted with challenging responsibilities in teaching and research so that they could have more opportunities to learn on the job and make better progress. Furthermore, some universities had established foundations to promote scholarship by younger faculty members (The Northeast College of Technology, 1988, and Yuan, 1988).

Another measure for the upgrading of university faculty was to grant generous academic leave. From the late 1970s to 1983, about 5 percent of university faculty members had been given a sabbatical leave for a one-year period (Huang, 1985). The 1985 *Decision of the CCP Central Committee on the Reform of the Educational System* endorsed this practice by stipulating that "where conditions permit, teachers, at and above the level of associate professor and assuming a relatively heavy teaching duty, should be given a year's leave every five years...." In fact, the extensive international exchange programs conducted by most colleges and universities had enabled many faculty members, at, below and above associate professor, to have extended leaves for overseas studies or research. It was not uncommon for some academic departments to have 30 percent of their faculty pursuing advanced studies and training or engaging in other scholarly activities at foreign universities (Sun, 1989, and Hu, 1989).

"Imparting Knowledge and Cultivating People"

With their social status reaffirmed and quality improved, faculty members at Chinese colleges and universities were expected to perform better both in teaching and in scholarship. In the realm of teaching, it was constantly emphasized that the faculty were duty-bound to train students who were to be "imbued with lofty aspirations, morally sound, well-disciplined" as well as professionally competent (CCP, 1985). In other words, faculty members should not just rest content with the transmission of knowledge and the training of skills. They were obliged, first and foremost, to act as role models for desirable student conduct. These obligations or dual responsibilities were aptly expressed in the slogan "imparting knowledge and cultivating people." With the growing student apathy to study and more frequent campus unrest, the dual responsibilities on the part of the faculty had been more persistently exhorted (Shen, 1990).

The rationale behind this concept and requirement was that a teaching position constituted more of a calling than a job. Answering the calling, a faculty member should, in addition to helping the students in their intellectual development, act as mentor and guide, cultivating the man first. This sense of calling was expected to be the center of the faculty members' professional identity and commitment.

In practice, multiple approaches had been advocated for the faculty to foster the students' moral as well as intellectual development. The most common was to integrate moral values into the course content so that these desirable values could be inculcated every hour of the day, six days a week, without an ostensible element of didactic indoctrination.

Faculty members were also expected to contribute to the moral growth of the students through a series of lectures covering a wide range of fields such as music, literature, fine arts and major, current domestic and international events. Additionally, faculty members were called upon to chair freewheeling discussions exploring multiple social issues about which the students were most concerned (*Yearbook*, p. 1129).

A more formalized approach to fostering the students' moral growth was to appoint faculty members as class teachers. In this role, the teachers served as counselors for students upon enrollment and before graduation when the students had the greatest need in counseling and other forms of help. (*Yearbook*, p. 1192).

These responsibilities charged to the faculty members made up an integral part of the expectations against which the faculty were measured in the evaluation for advancement in academic rank and for the consideration of advanced studies or training in foreign countries.

Academic Freedom

No discussion of the university faculty would be complete without some mention of academic freedom, which is essential to the creativity of the faculty, but had always been an elusive and sensitive issue in China. As already indicated, Chinese intellectuals were both utilized and distrusted. This ambivalence on the part of the CCP was characterized by the cycles of tightening and loosening of restrictions on intellectual activities. In the 1950s, the comparatively liberal and tolerant policy of the "Double Hundreds" was soon followed by the repression of candid opinions critical of the CCP and its bureaucrats. Although the policy claimed to encourage "a hundred flowers to blossom and a hundred schools of thought to contend" (Mao, 1957), the ensuing Anti-Rightist Campaign silenced and even persecuted those who had dared to speak out, let alone "contend." During the Cultural Revolution, which could be viewed as the culmination of all the previous political movements in the 1950s and early 1960s, the voice of only one "school" was heard and promoted.

In the markedly changed political climate after the Cultural Revolution, more tolerant policy guidelines were once again implemented. Following the removal of the stigma and the redressing of the false charges, intellectuals in China began to enjoy some ease of mind and a certain degree of freedom in their academic pursuits. Slogans such as "seeking truth from facts" and "practice as the sole criterion for testing truth" were constantly heard. The right to make hypotheses for natural scientists and freedom to engage in research, to publish and to design curricula not only emancipated the minds of intellectuals, but also rekindled their enthusiasm to serve the four modernization goals and to become part of the reform movements. As a result, scholarly journals multiplied, professional societies were established and numerous titles of books were published. For textbooks alone, 8000 titles were written or revised. Over 80 university presses were reactivated or established (Zhu, 1988).

Furthermore, outside employment that enhanced teaching and research was permitted, extra workloads were compensated for, and crowded living conditions began to be improved. On the whole, "Life for intellectuals in China has improved vastly in the past decade, in terms of both personal well-being and conditions conducive to creative work" (Hamrin, 1987).

The welcome and noticeable improvement of conditions for both life and work did not, however, mean the removal of all the restrictions. While creative academic pursuits were encouraged and promoted and administrative responsibilities entrusted, the Four Cardinal Principles had been insisted upon as the norm, from which no deviation was to be permitted.

The delicate nature of the issue of academic freedom naturally put university professors in a precarious position. But, having gone through numerous political movements and the turbulent years of the Cultural Revolution, they had committed themselves to the socialist system. Years of persistent political/ideological education and China's time-honored Confucian tradition of obedience more or less conditioned the Chinese intellectuals to restrictions of all descriptions. As long as their human dignity could be guaranteed and their right to engage in academic pursuits was not infringed upon, the Chinese intellectual would feel comfortable and content.

While this acceptance constituted the principal mind-set of most Chinese intellectuals, the vastly changed political context and the growing contact with the industrialized West had brought about increasing discontent of a few others. Lobbying for more changes, these people demanded the democratization of the whole political system in the hope that any issue, political or academic, could be brought up and debated. It was not certain whether or how long this radical advocation would be tolerated, but the fact that it was raised and made public was, in itself, a major event to be closely watched.

Summary

Like other intellectuals, the faculty of Chinese colleges and universities were subjected to thought remolding and injustices before the decade of reform and opening up. On the one hand, their expertise and contribution were deemed essential and utilized; on the other, their knowledge was regarded as a potential threat and, therefore, they were distrusted and discredited. As a result of the reform movement over the past decade, the intellectuals regained political influence and had their social status raised. By rhetoric at least, they had become an inalienable component of the working class indispensable to the nation's economic development.

With the regaining of political influence and the improvement of social status, the university faculty began to be promoted to appropriate academic ranks and granted a higher degree of freedom for creative teaching and scholarship. Under these favorable circumstances, much attention was devoted to professional development. The problems of inbreeding, low qualifications and the uneven age distribution of faculty members with the senior rank were, one by one, addressed and initially resolved. In connection with the higher political status and improved professional quality, the dual responsibilities of the university professors were emphasized. In addition to providing quality teaching and scholarship, the university professors were required to serve as role models and to help with the moral development of their students.

5

Students

"**F**aculty are the body of the university, but students are its lifeblood" (Fisher, 1984, p. 118). The professional development of faculty, the endeavor for academic freedom and the dual tasks of the faculty at Chinese institutions of higher learning were all primarily aimed at educating the students, who will be great assets indispensable to China's four modernization programs. As stated in the 1985 *Decision of the CCP Central Committee on the Reform of the Educational System*, Chinese institutions of higher learning were charged with the important task of training millions of educated, skilled and professionally competent workers for the nation's industry, agriculture, commerce and various other trades and professions. What changes, then, occurred with regard to the students at Chinese colleges and universities during the decade of reform and open-door policies?

To begin with, the enrollment system was revamped. The reinstatement of the unified national entrance examinations once again emphasized academic achievement. Instead of accepting students from among workers, peasants and soldiers for political considerations, institutions of higher learning began again to enroll high school graduates who had demonstrated adequate academic preparations through competitive examinations in all major high school subjects.

The revamped enrollment system also extended to graduate studies. After a suspension of 12 years, the universities began admitting and training large numbers of MA as well as PhD students. Connected with the revitalization of graduate programs, academic degrees began to be conferred for the first time since the founding of the People's Republic of China.

The second measure related to the students was the reform in the stipend system and, more significantly, in job assignment. Under the centrally formulated and controlled economic plans before the 1980s, most university students were given grants-in-aid for their studies, and all students were assigned a job upon graduation. In keeping with the economic and political reforms since the 1980s, scholarships and loans replaced the grants-in-aid. And the students would seek employment on their own instead of being automatically allocated a job upon completing their studies.

The last significant reform concerning the students was the vacillation of emphasis on "ideological and political work." With the progress and setbacks in China's reforms and the impact of Western ideas and values, the idealistic and inexperienced young college students became disenchanted and disoriented. For a time, they developed academic apathy and organized demonstrations for democracy and freedom. To modernize China but at the same time to uphold the much-exhorted Four Cardinal Principles, the CCP had initiated a variety of measures to imbue students "with lofty aspirations, moral integrity, sound academic grounding, and sense of discipline" (Liu, 1988).

Enrollment—Undergraduate Students

Prior to the Cultural Revolution, college students were selected from among senior high school graduates through unified national examinations. But during the Cultural Revolution, this practice was denounced as discriminatory against the children of blue-collar workers and farmers and subsequently abolished. When most colleges and universities reopened in 1972, a new selection system was introduced. Young workers, farmers and soldiers with a minimum of two years of work experience replaced senior high school graduates as candidates; peer recommendation and leadership approval replaced entrance examinations as criteria for selection. Political considerations took precedence over academic preparations. And many students thus enrolled were interested in Cultural Revolution politics rather than serious academic pursuits.

But this system was abandoned soon after the Cultural Revolution came to an end. Since 1978, the unified national entrance examinations had been reinstated. Each year, millions of senior high school graduates across China participated in the entrance examinations on the same days, in the same sequence and at the same time. Applicants for liberal arts took six subjects: politics, Chinese, mathematics, history, geography and a foreign language; applicants for engineering and natural sciences took seven: politics, Chinese, mathematics, physics, chemistry, biology and a foreign language. The choice of the foreign language was left to the students. Most would select English; some chose Russian or Japanese. A very small number might opt for French, German or Spanish.

After the examinations, the papers were collected by the provincial committees responsible for administering the college entrance examinations and graded by teachers drawn from institutions of higher learning and high schools. When the grading was completed, each province determined the minimum cutoff marks on the basis of the applicants' performance in the examinations. These cutoff marks would normally eliminate most of the applicants and leave only a small percentage of the candidates for selection by institutions of higher learning. At this point, institutions of higher learning sent their admissions officers to the designated city of each province where the files of the candidates were placed and made available for review.

The files of the candidates consisted of the candidates' applications, examination papers and scores, political evaluation, medical checkup results and high school grades. The students were considered for admission on the basis of their preferences of colleges and universities to attend, their performance in the entrance examinations and at high schools and the requirement and priority of the enrolling institutions. The students indicated their preferences in their applications, in which a number of schools and specialties were listed in rank order. Institutions often set minimum scores for certain subjects according to the requirements of their programs. In terms of priority, national-echelon, key institutions had the first choice of the candidates, followed by provincial, nonkey institutions and then three-year institutions and junior colleges. And correspondingly, candidates were divided into sections according to their total examination scores. Not until the candidates with higher scores had been admitted were the candidates with lower scores considered. Theoretically, the final decision of admission by an institution should be based on the all-around performance of candidates, which could be assessed from their files. But in practice, the entrance examination scores often constituted the principal determining factor. Only in borderline cases were other factors seriously considered.

To all appearances, this revived system of enrollment was a replica of the practice prior to the Cultural Revolution. But a careful study of the examinations and the enrollment process which had been constantly evolving since 1978 revealed a number of distinct differences.

These differences were first evident in the drafting of examination questions and the reforms in a number of other areas. To make sure that the best students were selected, the examinations stressed the validity and graduation of difficulty and added optional questions. And to avoid arbitrariness and disparity in the evaluation of the papers, standardized questions had increased from almost zero to an average of 50 percent (Shen, 1989).

These measures, however, did not eliminate the weakness of selecting students solely on the basis of the scores of a one-time examination. To remedy this problem, a comprehensive file with high school grades and the all-around evaluation of the students was requested from high schools. And for students applying for language studies, an oral/aural examination was added. More innovative than these, a joint graduation examination for all senior high school students was being piloted in Shanghai. The students who passed the joint examinations took college entrance examinations only in four subjects: Chinese, mathematics and two others related to the students' chosen fields of study. The scores of both sets of examinations were considered when the decision for admission was made (Liu, 1988). This pilot program was being perfected and would be field-tested in a number of other places (Liu).

Moreover, as part of the plan to relieve the dependence on the one-time entrance examinations, it was recommended that high school graduates who had excellent grades and also possessed a high degree of emotional maturity, ethical sensibility, creativity, aesthetic appreciation and a capacity to work effectively with others be admitted to colleges and universities without having to take the entrance examinations. Since 1987, 46 institutions of higher learning had begun to accept these students upon the recommendations by their schools (Wang, 1989). Also to minimize the weakness in the one-time entrance examinations, applicants with special talents but slightly lower than the minimum cutoff marks would be enrolled.

In addition, high school students in their junior years or even some elementary school graduates with exceptional scholastic achievements were recommended, selected and enrolled to study at colleges and universities. Since 1978, the Chinese University of Science and Technology in Hefei, Anhui Province, had enrolled nine groups of such "prodigies," who totaled 305 and ranged in age from 11 to 15. With custom-made courses for them, these students performed better academically than their older peers. Among the 145 graduates, 110 were making steady progress in their graduate studies, and 47 became PhD candidates in the United States and other countries. The success of this program at the Chinese University of Science and Technology prompted 12 more universities to establish similar programs (Wang, 1986). Each year, exceptionally gifted children would be extensively searched for, tested and accepted for enrollment by more and more colleges and universities.

One other feature that distinguished the enrollment in the recent decade from that during the 17 years prior to the Cultural Revolution was the obvious de-emphasis on the blood lineage of the students. Prior to the Cultural Revolution, students from the families of landlords, rich peasants, counterrevolutionaries, bad elements and anti-CCP Rightists were often denied the opportunity to study at colleges and universities, no matter how well they might have performed in college entrance examinations. A "Not Suitable for Admission" stamp on their applications would eliminate them for consideration at a very early stage of selection. This discriminatory practice was justified on the grounds that these categories of people were class enemies hostile to the CCP and the People's Republic of China. The children of these people would be strongly influenced by the deep-seated nonconforming beliefs and attitudes of their parents or even grandparents. Unless these children underwent a thorough thought remolding and broke away from their families, which would be a protracted struggle, they could not have genuine allegiance to the CCP and the new regime.

When China shifted its emphasis from class struggle to economic development, this theory was repudiated, and the class line was obliterated. The students began to be judged for their own qualifications, no longer by their family origins. In other words, the long-advocated dictum of "everyone being equal before the marks" in college enrollment had at last become possible (Wang, 1990).

Though class origin ceased to be a major factor in college enrollment, tertiary institutions still insisted on pronounced political criteria for the applicants. These included the adherence to the Four Cardinal Principles and the observance of disciplines and laws. But in practice, almost all senior high school graduates who did not have a police record were eligible for examination and admission.

The enrollment system in the decade from 1978 to 1988 also differed from the pre-Cultural Revolution practice in that additional students could be admitted through multiple channels beyond the plan mandated by the state. With the enlarged decision-making power, institutions of higher learning began in 1983 to enroll students at the request of employers, with over 3200 of these students enrolled in that year by contracts between institutions of higher learning and government agencies or enterprises. In 1987, more than 25,000 of this type of students were enrolled (Li, 1988).

In addition, self-financing students began to be enrolled in 1985. Insofar as their teaching capacities permitted, institutions of higher learning began to have the authority to admit students who had reached minimum cutoff scores and agreed to pay all the expenses, including tuition and miscellaneous fees. In 1987, 14,000 such students were enrolled, which made up 3 percent of the year's total enrollment (Li, 1988).

These two means through which more students were enrolled helped to tap the potential of colleges and universities, thus increasing the cost-effectiveness and also promoting curricular reforms. These measures "fit in with the reform of China's economic management system and the development of market regulation and, therefore, have great vitality and broad prospects for development" (Wei, 1984). They particularly benefitted small, township enterprises which had had great difficulty obtaining much-needed technical personnel.

Enrollment—Graduate Students

Parallel with the enrollment of undergraduate students, graduate enrollment in China also experienced continuous reforms in the new decade. Restored in 1978 after a hiatus of 12 years, the enrollment of graduate students numbered 110,000 in 1988, 159 times the 1949 figure (*Guangming Daily,* September 22, 1989, p. 2). These graduate students pursued MA and PhD studies full-time or part-time at institutions of higher learning and independent research institutes under the Chinese Academy of Sciences (CAS) and the Chinese Academy of Social Sciences (CASS).

The entrance examinations for MA students consisted of a preliminary and a final. The preliminary included examinations on political theories and on a foreign language prepared by the SEC and three examinations on other areas in the applicants' disciplines designed by individual institutions. The final test was conducted in the form of an interview. Outstanding applicants were also recommended for master's-level studies without having to take the entrance examinations.

The entrance examinations for PhD students were similar to those for MA applicants. But the number and content of the examinations, both oral and written, in the applicants' disciplines were determined and prepared entirely by individual institutions instead of the SEC. In addition, the applicants had to have the recommendation of two scholars at or above the level of associate professor.

Political dependability, as reflected in the conformity with the Four Cardinal Principles, and physical fitness constituted other criteria for the enrollment of MA and PhD students. In addition, there was an age requirement of 35 for MA and 40 for PhD applicants. To improve the quality of graduate education, a two-year work experience was desired, particularly in the field of applied sciences and liberal arts. The BA recipients with five years of practical experience and outstanding contributions had priority in admission (SEC, 1988, p. 112). To ensure that a growing number of students had some practical experience before they began to pursue graduate studies, many universities such as Qinghua in Beijing arranged for the newly admitted graduate students to work for two to five years before they commenced their graduate studies (Gung, 1988).

Academic Degrees

Until 1980, graduates from Chinese colleges and universities received a diploma which certified the completion of undergraduate studies. The few students who had taken master's-level graduate education received no degrees. With the renewed emphasis on serious academic pursuits and the rapid development of graduate education, the Standing Committee of the National People's Congress drew up and ratified *The Regulations Governing Academic Degrees of the PRC* and put it into effect in January 1981. According to the Regulations, "any Chinese citizen who upholds the leadership of the Communist Party of China, supports the socialist system and attains a certain academic level" was eligible for BA, MA, or PhD degrees.

The graduates who had fulfilled all the requirements of a four-year curriculum and had been approved for graduation would receive the bachelor's degree. These graduates must complete all the course work and a thesis and demonstrate a satisfactory command of the basic theories, knowledge and skills of their fields of study as well as some ability to undertake scientific research or to engage in technical work. The BA degree was conferred simultaneously with a diploma certifying the completion of the undergraduate studies. But not every diploma was accompanied by the BA degree.

Students who had successfully completed two to three years of graduate studies and passed a written examination in the prescribed courses along with an oral defense of their thesis would receive the MA degree. These candidates must demonstrate a firm grasp of the basic theories and systematic knowledge in their field of study and an ability for scientific research and for technical work. Those who undertook master's-level studies at institutions unauthorized to confer MA degrees could apply to receive the degree from the institutions whose MA programs had been accredited by the National Academic Committee under the State Council.

Students who had a solid, comprehensive grasp of the basic theories and systematic, specialized knowledge in their branch of learning would receive their doctoral degree. The candidates must demonstrate a reading, research and writing ability in one foreign language and a reading, research ability in a second foreign language. They must pass written examinations in the prescribed courses before an oral examination of the dissertation. The oral examination board would consist of five to seven professors or specialists with the senior academic rank. Of these members, two or three must be from other institutions. A two-thirds majority must be obtained by secret ballot before the degree could be conferred. The doctoral dissertation was usually published.

The applicants for the doctoral degree who had published important works, made original scientific discoveries and rendered significant contributions to science and technology could be exempt from part or all of the course examinations.

The Regulations Governing Academic Degrees of the PRC also stipulated that honorary doctoral degrees could be conferred on distinguished Chinese and foreign scholars. In addition, in-service faculty members and research personnel who possessed equivalent qualifications and had passed the examinations on required courses and oral examinations on the thesis or dissertation were eligible to apply for corresponding degrees.

As of 1988, 545 institutions of higher learning and research institutes in China were accredited to confer MA degrees in 6407 disciplines, 238 institutions of higher learning and research institutes were accredited to confer PhD degrees in 1830 disciplines and 3798 professors and research fellows were authorized as academic advisors for PhD students (*Guangming Daily,* September 22, 1989, p. 2). By 1987, 53,300 MA, 664 PhD and 36 honorary doctoral degrees had been conferred in China (SEC, 1989, p. 34).

Financial Aid

In keeping with its centrally planned economic development policy, China established in the early 1950s not only a unified enrollment and job assignment system, but also a financial aid package whereby the state paid almost all the educational and living expenses of the students, which included tuition, on-campus accommodation and medical care. Students who had difficulty paying for board were given grants-in-aid, with the amount determined on the basis of the income of the students' families. These financial-aid policies were necessary at the time for the training of high-level specialists urgently needed to recover and build up the nation's economic strength and for assisting the children from worker and peasant families to study at institutions of higher learning. The policies were also feasible at the time, because the number of institutions and student enrollment were both very small.

However, the adverse effects of these financial responsibilities on the part of the state became apparent as the nation's political and economic reforms deepened. The all-inclusive government responsibility discouraged the students from striving and competing for excellence and caused them to become too dependent on the state. Furthermore, with the rapid increase in the number of institutions and in enrollment, the state could no longer afford the cost.

To overcome these defects, the CCP decided to replace the grants-in-aid with scholarships and loans beginning from the students enrolled in 1987 (Liu, 1987). The scholarships were awarded to three categories of students. Those with commendable academic, political and moral records were graded in terms of excellence, with the highest grade being given to the top 5 percent of students, the second grade to the next 10 percent and the third to the following 10 percent. Also eligible for the scholarship were students majoring in agriculture, forestry, geology, mining, physical education and others who would work in tough conditions, along with the students at teacher-training institutions. Other students who qualified for scholarships were those who committed themselves to work upon graduation in remote and underdeveloped regions.

In addition to the scholarships, which provided awards for academic excellence and for commitment to certain professions and regions, low-interest loans were made available to the students in need on the condition of repayment. It was stipulated that when the graduates were employed, the loans would be repaid in a lump sum by the employer. The employer, in turn, would deduct the money from the salaries of these graduates each month over a five-year period. Here again, incentives were offered. Graduates who were willing to teach at elementary and secondary schools or to work in economically backward regions and in professions with harsh conditions would be exempt from the repayment of loans.

Besides the abolition of the grants-in-aid, some long-term and drastic reform measures such as the charge of tuition and fees were being considered (Zhu, 1988). But due to the complexity of the problem, no concrete plans had been announced.

Job Assignment

More significant and complex than the reforms in financial aid, according to educational leaders in China, was the job assignment system for university graduates (Zhu, 1988). As with the freshmen-enrollment system, the job assignment for graduates had been highly centralized before the 1980s. Each year, a detailed placement plan would be mandated from the central government, leaving little flexibility for the institutions of higher learning and few choices for the students. When the placement plan was transmitted, the institutions began to allocate their graduating students to designated places and positions. And the students were constantly admonished to "subordinate their own needs to those of the state, obey the assignment and go wherever they are needed" (Hu and Seifman, 1987, p. 125).

This system worked well with the centralized control of the nation's economic development before the 1980s. But with the increasing decentralization of power and the burgeoning market regulation in the economy since the 1980s, incongruities and conflicts became evident and frequent. Government agencies and state-owned enterprises were often supplied with more people than they needed, while most other places, especially small, township industries, could not obtain a single college graduate in spite of their more urgent need (Chen, 1987). Moreover, unable to choose their own employment but still assured a job, many students were not as dedicated and motivated as they should have been in their studies.

To solve these problems, the SEC introduced a variety of measures for pilot or field tests over recent years. For example, it began to provide general guidelines instead of issuing mandatory plans. Much latitude was given to colleges and universities to work out specific placement arrangements in consultation with prospective employers. Upon the approval of the SEC, these jointly finalized plans would be released to the students, who were then asked to indicate their preference for assignment.

One other measure for field test was the introduction of a "two-way choice." In place of the arbitrary assignment of graduates to employers, institutions of higher learning invited employers to campus to meet with the graduates and allowed the students to choose their jobs under the guidance of the state placement plans. One year before the students graduated, colleges and universities sent letters to potential employers, briefing them on the academic standing of the students and asking about the needs of the employers. The information thus gained was made available to the students, who subsequently filled in job application forms. Then, the institutions arranged meetings between the employers and the students. During these meetings, the students learned more about the prospective job requirements, fringe benefits and working and housing conditions (wage scales in China were fixed, and it was customary for employers to provide housing for employees). Also during these meetings, the employers further examined the applicants' qualifications.

More radical than these "two-way choice" meetings, which had to operate within the boundary of the placement guidelines set by the state, graduates began to be permitted to seek positions on their own. They could write letters of application to prospective employers and make personal contacts in order to secure a position of their independent choice.

Though these reforms were not yet made universal due to wide social complications of the job assignment system, initial reaction had been very favorable, and much success had been reported. Compared with previous years, more graduates had gone to work in places where they felt they could put their knowledge and expertise to fuller use and make greater contributions. More graduates had gone to grass-roots organizations and township- or village-run enterprises where they were more urgently needed (Qu, 1988).

Following the success of these initial reform measures, the SEC decided that beginning from the students enrolled in 1989, the state-controlled system of job assignment would be on the whole abolished. Except for government placement for teaching professions, occupations with harsh working conditions and remote regions, most students would be able to apply for positions upon the recommendation of their colleges and universities. But to guarantee employment for every qualified graduate, institutions of higher learning would still help those who might fail to obtain employment on their own (Zhu, 1988).

Academic Apathy and the Students' State of Mind

It is widely believed in the West that Chinese college students are highly intelligent and diligent (Rosemont, 1985; Jacobs, 1988; Craig, 1989; Richardson, 1989; Pretzer, 1989). Recounting his experience teaching at Fudan University as a Fulbright scholar, Rosemont wrote:

> Linguistics students in one class mastered a symbolic logic text (in English) in less than a month; philosophy graduates have grappled effectively with Wittgenstein's *Tractatus*, and their peers in political theory with John Rawls' *A Theory of Justice*. [1985]

Both the intelligence and hard-working spirit of the college students in China were to be expected. In a country where after careful screening only about 10 percent of the applicants could get into traditional colleges and universities, it was only natural that these young people were the nation's best and brightest. And it was taken for granted that they should treasure this rare opportunity and continue to excel in their academic endeavors.

However, a discernible trend of academic weariness developed during the 1980s. Instead of applying themselves in their studies as they should have, many college students slackened their efforts and became content with only mediocre results. A survey conducted in 1988 of Fudan University students showed that between eight and ten in the evening when all students were supposed to be busy with their studies, only 40 percent were actually studying. Of the rest of the students, 10 percent were engaging in casual talk. Ten percent were watching television or movies. Seven percent were with their girl- or boyfriends, and the remainder were "otherwise occupied" (Li, 1989).

This lethargy in academic pursuits was not limited to Fudan. At a university in Wuhan, for instance, absenteeism reached as high as 35 percent (Li and Liu, 1989). On the door of a residence hall on the Beijing University campus hung a slogan which read "The sea of knowledge is infinite. Only by turning back can you come to the shore of paradise" (Li, 1989). On most campuses, students' goals in their academic studies were no more than a 60 percent passing mark. In addition, cheating became common and no longer stigmatized.

More distressing than the lethargy, undergraduate and graduate students began to abandon their studies and to drop out. In 1988, over 6000 undergraduate and 2000 graduate students discontinued their programs, at a dropout rate of 0.32 and 1.8 percent respectively (The State Statistical Bureau, 1989). Although the rate was insignificant, it represented the beginning of a phenomenon which had virtually been nonexistent in China. And it was occurring at an accelerated rate.

Equally disturbing was the decreasing numbers of applicants for graduate studies. At some institutions, there began to be fewer applicants than slots (Zhou, 1988). In many cases, only those who were eager to move out of less desirable occupations, institutions or regions applied for graduate studies. Thus, graduate studies were becoming a means for upward social and geographical mobility, which was not otherwise possible, rather than a passion for academic achievements.

With the loss of interest in serious academic pursuits, a business fervor soon appeared on campus. In addition to the officially approved part-study, part-work programs, students set up stalls working as peddlers and cafe bosses or attendants. Many tried their hands as salespeople for state-owned factories or private enterprises. Some even started their own companies engaging in the transaction of a variety of scarce and expensive items or commodities (*Xinguancha*, 1989).

The proliferation of these business endeavors further diverted students from their studies. "The Yellow Path," a term which was coined to describe a coveted, lucrative career in business, became the mind-set of a considerable number of the student entrepreneurs. "The Red Path," a term which was used to denote a government position with security and power, lost its erstwhile glamour and appeal. The least favored was "the Black Path," which meant the gowns, the "dark alley" of academia.

A major reason for this increasing academic boredom and escalating business fervor lay in the discriminatory remuneration for college graduates. In China, intellectuals were generally not well paid. According to a 1988 survey of Beijing residents, the average salaries for white-collar workers were lower than those for blue-collar workers. Among people of the same age, the less education one had, the more one was paid. The intellectuals who had been through college were paid 21.3 percent less than those who had education at the level of junior high school or even lower (Lu, 1989). Another survey, which was conducted nationwide among young people, indicated that in terms of economic rewards, individual laborers ranked first whereas university graduates were placed in the ninth position among eleven occupations (Bai, 1987).

While this "inverse order" in the remunerations for mental and manual workers contributed to the academic apathy, it would be unfair to assume that China's college students in the 1980s became materialistic and uninterested in wider social issues. The academic apathy and business fervor constituted, to a certain extent, a conscious reaction to the corruption and bureaucracy of a few CCP and government officials. In addition, many students took the opportunity of running businesses as a means to adapt themselves to the environment, to test their knowledge and expertise and to experience firsthand a genuine, fair competition.

In fact, most college students had a keen awareness of their social responsibilities, and searched for the best ways to build up China. But having not been humbled by life or learned its necessary limitations, these young, exuberant students often had exalted notions. And their youthful vigor and enthusiasm were tainted with idealism and inflated egos.

The students' awareness of social responsibilities was reflected in their concern for reform issues and in their eagerness to participate in the reforms. After a period of confusion and search for identity in the late 1970s, the students were inspired by the CCP's shift of emphasis from class struggle to extensive economic development. The subsequent successes of rural reforms and the prospects of political restructuring in the early 1980s further enthused these college students, who made up their minds to join in the national efforts for a modern, prosperous China. Students in Beijing, for example, advanced slogans such as "Unite to revitalize China" and "Start now and start with ourselves." To contribute their share to the deepening reforms, these students formed discussion groups, organized seminars, went out of their campuses to investigate and study wider social issues and volunteered to work after graduation at grass-roots levels and in remote or economically underdeveloped regions (Li, 1988, and Cheng, 1989).

In their discussions about and participation in the reforms, college students reflected over the future of China and searched for ways to accelerate the pace of China's modernization process. For this purpose, they studied, compared and absorbed different ideas: Chinese as well as Western; orthodox as well as unorthodox. For brief periods of time, Sartre and Nietzsche became their favorite writers. And later, other Western ideas and values such as political pluralism, democracy and freedom appealed to them. Indignant with the malpractice among a handful of CCP and government officials and disillusioned by other problems which had cropped up in the reform process, college students began to doubt the much-advocated superiority of the socialist system and to question the legitimacy of CCP leadership. Surveys between 1986 and 1988 in Beijing showed that a growing number of students held that a multiple-party system and capitalism would be viable alternatives for the future of China (Cheng, 1989).

In their enthusiasm for the reforms and the search for viable alternatives for their motherland, college students considered themselves to be "the natural advocates" and pioneers (Wu, 1989, and Qiao, 1989). Taking pride in being the few elites or, as the Chinese saying went, "God's most favored sons," they harbored unrealistic hopes for the reforms, thinking that China would change overnight. When tangible, welcome achievements were made, they tended to feel elated. But in the face of setbacks and complications, they would quickly become frustrated and dispirited. Due to their idealism and inexperience, they soon became impatient, craving immediate results from the reforms, only to be more disillusioned. This revolution of rising expectations led, in part, to a massive outbreak of demonstrations sweeping about

150 campuses in 17 cities in December 1986 and January 1987 (Stavis, 1988, p. 89), the most extensive student agitation since the Cultural Revolution. These demonstrations provided an outlet for the students' pent-up emotions and an opportunity to make their voices heard. But the revolt contributed little to solving the myriad problems in China except the resignation of the then CCP General Secretary Hu Yaobang, who was one of the most reform-minded leaders of the CCP. During the subsequent two years, problems in China's reforms continued to mount up, and college students became more agonized and defiant. Another wave of demonstrations of an explosive magnitude was to be expected.

"Strengthening Ideological and Political Work"

The CCP adopted a conciliatory stance toward the 1986/87 student demonstrations. Ascribing the agitation to the pernicious influence of bourgeois liberalism, the CCP tolerated it by stating that "The students demonstrated out of their concern for the reform and their good intentions to accelerate the advance of the socialist democratization. Their enthusiasm is understandable" (*China Daily,* December 25, 1986, p. 4).

But the toleration of the demonstrations did not mean the abandoning of the Four Cardinal Principles, which constituted the parameters for China's reforms and, in fact, every aspect of Chinese life. In higher education, these principles translated into the training of advanced, specialized personnel "with lofty aspirations, moral integrity, sound academic grounding and sense of discipline" (Liu, 1988).

To reach this goal, the CCP strengthened its "ideological and political work" among the college students by adopting a number of measures. Most notable among these were the reform of the required courses in political theories, the addition of a moral education course, the requirement and organization of social practice and the reintroduction of compulsory military training.

Traditionally, the curriculum for Chinese colleges and universities had consisted of four compulsory courses in political theories: the History of the CCP, Political Economy, Philosophy and International Communist Movement. These courses took up an average of 15 percent of the class hours for all types of institutions of higher learning. With the changed situation in the 1980s, the CCP began a planned, gradual reform in these courses and introduced a new curriculum in political theories. In 1988, most colleges and universities inaugurated courses in the history of the Chinese revolution and courses in the development of Chinese socialism. And it was expected that in 1990, colleges and universities would offer courses in basic principles of Marxism-Leninism. These courses were believed to be more relevant to Chinese circumstances and would address many of the current issues in China. The courses in the basic principles of Marxism-Leninism aimed to provide the students with a full realization of the scientific nature of Marxism, of its truth and of its importance as a set of guiding principles. It was claimed that with a firm grasp of the Marxist-Leninist principles, the students would no longer have doubts and conflicting thoughts when confronted with the inundation of Western ideas and values (Zhu, 1990).

The class-hour or credit-hour requirement for these courses varied from institution to institution. But it was stipulated that the courses in the basic principles of Marxism-Leninism alone required 210 class hours (Zhu).

In addition to the reformed curriculum in political theories, a new course in moral education had been introduced, and a faculty for the specific purpose of moral education was being developed. This was an ad hoc course aiming at instilling Communist ideas and ideals, moral concepts and aesthetic sensibilities into the minds of students. The classes included formal lectures, seminars, devotional assemblies as well as informal counseling sessions and extracurricular activities.   To link these on-campus classes for ideological education with a broad social experience, the CCP required that college students engage in social practice or investigations during summer and winter vacations. According to a report in the *Guangming Daily,* the nation's leading paper for intellectuals, this required program had been "popularized and regularized" (March 15, 1987, p. 3). During the summer vacation of 1987, over one million students from 1000 colleges and universities participated in these activities in many parts of the country. Many institutions had chosen specific areas as stable bases for their students' social studies. Almost all institutions had made these programs part of the required courses; some had even assigned fixed credit hours for these programs (*Guangming Daily*).

The programs in social studies also extended to high schools. Beginning in 1988, students who had not had these experiences would not be eligible to apply for college admission.

Besides the required social contacts and studies, the CCP reinvigorated military training for college students. A directive jointly issued in 1985 by a number of government ministries and the PLA's General Staff Department stated that the purposes of conducting military training among students were to strengthen reserve forces, train reserve officers, heighten the students' political consciousness and patriotic sentiments and increase the students' sense of discipline. The military training was conducted either on university campuses or in army barracks. The length of the training varied from eight weeks to six months, and the grades of the training were entered in the students' report cards (*Circular on Military Training at Selected Schools* and Guan, 1988).

Summary

Soon after the Cultural Revolution ended, the unified college entrance examinations were restored. Instead of accepting workers, peasants and soldiers as students on the basis of peer recommendations, colleges and universities once again admitted students from among high school graduates on the basis of academic achievements. To overcome the overdependence on the one-time examination scores, colleges and universities also considered a number of other factors, such as the applicant's high school grades, special talents and political awareness, in making final admission decisions. Students with outstanding, all-around development could go to universities without having to take the unified entrance examinations.

Along with the resumption of college entrance examinations, graduate studies were reactivated after a suspension of 12 years. While the enrollment of undergraduate students in 1988 doubled that of 1978, the enrollment of graduate students showed a tenfold increase during the same period.

With the renewed emphasis on academic achievements and the rapid development of graduate studies, China began to confer academic degrees for the first time since the founding of PRC in 1949. Since 1981, all qualified graduates from undergraduate and graduate programs had been awarded BA, MA and PhD degrees.

One other reform with regard to students was the replacement of stipends with scholarships and loans and the plan of charging tuition and fees. These measures were aimed at encouraging the students to excel in their academic pursuits and at lessening the financial burden of the government.

More significant and complex than the financial reform was the job assignment for graduating students. Since the early 1950s, all college and university graduates had been assigned a job upon graduation. But during the 1980s, a mutual choice system was piloted and field-tested. The prospective employers could choose from a pool of job applicants, and the graduates were given the freedom to select their employment. Beginning in 1993, all college and university students would seek their own employment.

China's ongoing social, economic and political reforms also brought about problems among college and university students. One of the most serious among them was academic apathy. Instead of exerting themselves in their studies as before, many students pursued pleasure, and some engaged in businesses of all descriptions. In a sense, these phenomena might be considered a conscious reaction against many of China's social problems. Eager to contribute to the nation's reforms but unprepared for the complexities of the reforms, these young, idealistic students became impatient, craving immediate results. Their sense of responsibility and the frustrations they had experienced led to an outbreak of massive demonstrations in major Chinese cities during December 1986 and January 1987.

The CCP tolerated these demonstrations, but it continued to enforce the Four Cardinal Principles and had taken a number of measures to train students with "lofty aspirations, moral integrity, sound academic grounding and sense of discipline." Most significant among these approaches were the reform in the courses of political theories, the initiation of a moral education program, the requirement of social practice and the formalization of compulsory military training.

6

Exchanges with Other Countries

"**N**ational seclusion cannot lead to modernization" (CCP, 1984). To build up a modern, strong and prosperous China, Chinese authorities at various times attached great importance to scholarly and academic exchanges with foreign countries, especially with the industrialized West. As early as the late nineteenth century, the government of the Qing Dynasty sent a considerable number of scholars and students to the United States and to some European countries in search of Western learning to strengthen China's economy and to prevent China from falling prey to the aggression and subjugation of invading foreign powers. At the beginning of the twentieth century, large numbers of students went to Japan, studying at about 60 schools. Accepting scholarships from the Boxer Indemnity established by the American government in 1909, several thousand Chinese students went to the United States. In 1918 alone, 1124 Chinese students pursued studies in 73 disciplines at American colleges and universities (Wu, 1985). At about the same time, many Chinese went to France on work-study programs and to the Soviet Union for the study of socialism. During the 1950s and early 1960s, the Communist government sent over 10,000 students and scholars primarily to the Soviet Union and East European countries (*Guangming Daily,* September 22, 1989, p. 2). These students and scholars majored in a wide range of disciplines from "aerodynamics to zoology" (Reed, 1988, p. 89).

In varying degrees, all these study-abroad programs accelerated China's development in science and technology and promoted the transition of China from a backward, feudal society into a modern, democratic society.

But these programs were discontinued during the early period of the Cultural Revolution. For five years, no students or scholars were dispatched to other countries for advanced studies or research. Beginning in 1972 when foreign exchanges resumed and in 1976 when the Cultural Revolution ended, only 1629 students were sent to the UK, West Germany, France, Canada and Japan. And the majority of these students majored in the study of languages (Huang, 1987).

Since the strategic shift of emphasis in the late 1970s from class struggle to economic development, study-abroad programs had become an integral part of China's policy of opening to the outside world (SEC, 1987). China began sending larger numbers of students and scholars than ever before for advanced studies and training in foreign countries. From 1978 to 1988, approximately 60,000 students and scholars were selected and sent to 76 countries and regions. In addition, about 20,000 students went to foreign countries for education at their own expense (*Guangming Daily,* September 22, 1989, p. 2).

This record number of students and scholars for overseas studies and training between 1978 and 1988 constituted the major part of China's international exchanges in education, science and culture. Other forms of exchange with foreign countries consisted of accepting overseas students for advanced studies in China, exchanging visiting professors, pursuing cooperative research, exchanging delegations, establishing partnerships between institutions and participating in and organizing   international symposia (Huang, 1987).

Since the sending of students and scholars made up the predominant form of China's scholarly and academic exchanges with foreign countries, this chapter will concentrate on the development of policies, the problem of brain drain, the utilization of returned students and scholars and other problems associated with these study-abroad programs in the last decade. And since two-thirds of the Chinese students and scholars studying or working overseas were in the United States, and China led all the other countries and regions in the number of its students in the United States (*Chronicle of Higher Education,* November 22, 1989, p. A25), this chapter will also discuss China's brain-drain problem vis-à-vis the United States.

Evolving Policies

The Cultural Revolution debilitated China's higher education and scientific research and widened the already narrowed gap between China and other countries in many areas of education (CCP, 1985). To change this backwardness and catch up with other countries, Deng Xiaoping stated that "science and technology are part of the wealth created in common by all mankind" and emphasized that it should be a long-term strategic policy for China to "increase international academic exchanges" and to expand "contacts and cooperations with scientific circles in other countries" (1984). Deng's advocation was endorsed by the CCP and the nation and was quickly translated into concrete action. In 1978, the Ministry of Education issued a circular with specific policies for the expansion of study-abroad programs. The document stipulated that undergraduate students, graduate students and visiting scholars should be selected and sent in increasing numbers to study science, engineering, agriculture, medicine and a host of other subjects. Undergraduate students should be selected from college freshmen; graduate students should be selected from those newly enrolled in higher education and research institutions for graduate studies and visiting scholars should be selected from among the mid-career university professors, researchers and other technical personnel.

In 1979, a total of 1750 people were selected from Chinese colleges and universities for studies and research at foreign universities. Of these people, 335 (19 percent) were undergraduates, 117 (7 percent) were graduate students and 1298 (74 percent) were faculty members. Among the faculty members, the younger went for advanced studies and training in their fields of study, and the older went as visiting scholars to renew their knowledge and expertise (SEC, 1989, p. 91).

In subsequent years, several national conferences were convened to review the study-abroad programs and to make policy adjustments that would better match China's changing needs and circumstances.

These policy adjustments were first reflected in the composition of the people for study or training at foreign institutions of higher learning. During the late 1970s and early 1980s, more visiting scholars were selected and sent, as China was eager to overcome the debilitating effect of the Cultural Revolution on its higher education. These visiting scholars were mostly middle-aged faculty members who had survived the Cultural Revolution but had fallen behind in their fields of study. It was hoped that with renewed knowledge, these faculty members would help to revitalize China's higher education by improving the quality of teaching and research. In the mid-1980s, the visiting scholars began to return upon completion of their studies and to assume important teaching and research responsibilities. From then on, more graduate students were selected and dispatched for MA or PhD studies. In 1984, for example, out of a total of 3830 people sponsored by the government, 1564 were graduate students, a 37 percent increase over 1979. The number of faculty members sent as visiting scholars showed a considerable drop over the same period (SEC, p. 91).

With the rapid development of China's own master's and doctoral programs in the late 1980s, a change in the composition of the candidates for studies at foreign universities took place. Instead of sending large numbers of master's and doctoral students as before, China shifted its emphasis to postdoctoral and research scholars, who would have short visits to keep themselves abreast of the latest developments in their fields. According to Chinese authorities, there were several advantages in sending these two categories of people. As they would spend a relatively short period of time abroad, more could be sent in rapid succession. Moreover, the scholars who had made a career start and had a family back in China had a larger stake than young students in returning upon completion of their programs, and when they returned, they would resume their former positions without having to rely on the government for job assignments.

Another policy adjustment was reflected in the increased channels for foreign-study programs. Besides sending an average of 3000 students and scholars on national programs, the Chinese government had been encouraging institutions of higher learning to develop and establish partnerships with their foreign counterparts. These institutional cooperations made it possible for a much larger number of students and scholars to study or engage in research at foreign universities. Since 1978, 186 Chinese institutions of higher learning had established these partnerships with 398 colleges and universities in over 40 countries. Mainly through these exchanges, about 5000 students and scholars were given the opportunity to study overseas each year (SEC, p. 94).

More liberal and significant than these institutional-exchange programs were the evolving policies concerning students applying for studies in foreign universities at their own expense. When the Chinese government first allowed students to study abroad at their own expense in 1981, it enforced no restrictions as long as the applicants could provide evidence of sufficient financial support in hard currency or foreign scholarships as well as evidence of admission by foreign colleges and universities. After 1982, some restrictions began to be imposed. For example, college students were no longer allowed to discontinue their studies in China. Also, they had to work for two years after graduation before they were permitted to apply for self-financed studies at foreign universities. But these restrictions were soon removed. Toward the end of 1984, the State Council announced:

> All Chinese citizens who are able to secure financial support in foreign currency
> or foreign scholarships through proper means and who have gained admission
> to foreign educational institutions can apply for undergraduate or graduate

studies at their own expense regardless of former education, age, or length of employment. [*Chinese Education*, 1988, p. 25]

This highly liberal policy opened the floodgate for Chinese students to go abroad for undergraduate as well as graduate studies. Many of them began to devote much time and energy to preparing for the TOEFL at the expense of their normal studies. Some even dropped out of colleges and universities. The "overseas study fever," which had already been pervasive in China, was intensified. According to Yu Fuzeng, Director of the Foreign Affairs Bureau under the SEC, 80 percent of graduate students at some national, key universities spent much time seeking ways to secure foreign funding, preparing for TOEFL and writing letters of application to foreign universities (1989). For a time, China's own undergraduate and graduate education was seriously disrupted. And Chinese colleges and universities faced the danger of becoming "prep schools" for the students whose "major objective in life" was to attend overseas universities and to obtain foreign degrees (Xiao, 1986).

This interference with the development of China's own higher education was extensively discussed at a 1986 national conference, which resulted in the drafting and promulgation of comprehensive CCP regulations governing the study-abroad programs. Concerning self-financed students, the document promised continued moral support and equal political treatment, but prohibited graduate students from interrupting their studies. The document stipulated that the graduate students must complete their studies at home institutions before they were permitted to go overseas for further studies. And when they finally gained permission to go overseas, their studies would be incorporated into the programs of the sending institutions. This meant that while overseas, their tenure and salary would be retained, and that they would be obligated to return upon completing their studies overseas. University lecturers, engineers, physicians-in-charge and other people who were classified as essential to their work units and to China were not allowed to study abroad at their own expense. They could only go on institutional programs.

Other policy adjustments included the diversification of student destinations. To expose its students and scholars to the scientific and technological strengths of as many countries as possible, the Chinese government planned not to have the government-sponsored students and scholars go only to the United States. Instead, it decided to send the majority of these people to countries that "are capable of accepting more, but have taken few so far" (Huang, 1988). Of the 3000 students and scholars on government programs each year, about 20 percent would be sent to the United States, 50 percent to Europe, 20 percent to Australia, and 10 percent to Japan (Reed, 1988, p. 103).

Besides planning to redirect the student flow, the SEC improved the planning and selection of candidates for study-abroad programs. Better planning entailed that students and scholars should be sent to foreign universities according to the needs of China's social and economic developments and the needs of the sending institutions. In other words, the emphasis would be on disciplines in which China had a shortage and which were most important for China's modernization.

In addition, a more direct link between foreign education and the specific needs of the sponsoring institutions was emphasized. To ensure the link, the students and scholars going to study in foreign countries were requested to enter into agreements with their sponsoring institutions specifying the objectives and subjects of the study-abroad programs along with the rights, obligations and the responsibilities of both the sponsoring institutions and the students and scholars. Efforts were also made to guide the self-financed students so that they would pursue advanced studies in line with China's needs (SEC, 1987).

The improvement of selection meant that the students and scholars chosen for studies overseas must meet more stringent standards. In addition to demonstrating professional capability, language proficiency and physical fitness, they must love their motherland, support socialism, possess moral integrity and have a strong work ethic. In the words of He Dongchang, Minister-in-Charge of the SEC, China did not want to send its best and brightest overseas, only to have them turn against their own country and socialism (1989).

Clearly, these modifications and adjustments of policies were not meant to limit or reduce the study-abroad programs. Rather, they were measures to improve the selection of candidates and the management of the programs so that China could have maximum benefit. With the revitalization and development of Chinese higher education, the shift from scholars to students and back to scholars as principal candidates for foreign-study programs was understandable and rational. To maintain the dynamics of China's own graduate education, it was not unreasonable to adopt a few protective measures. And to have a fuller spectrum of foreign technologies and to avoid being too dependent on one source, it was necessary to diversify China's contacts to reach more countries. Some of the policy stipulations, such as signing agreements, were resented by students and scholars. But the practice was customary in many developing countries. In China, it was not only a means for better planning and supervision, but also a measure to guarantee the return of its much-needed scientific and professional manpower. To realize the goals of the Four Modernizations, China must not lose too many of its best and brightest (Wang, 1989).

But due to the sensitive nature of the study-abroad programs, these policies and their constant adjustments gave rise to flurries of confusion, rumor, misgivings and even fear among the Chinese, especially those who were eligible for advanced studies at foreign universities. To clarify the issues and allay the misgivings and fear, high-level Chinese officials gave extensive interviews and made repeated statements. In his lengthy interview with reporters from China's official Xinhua news agency, Liu Zhongde, Deputy Minister of the SEC, explained in detail the policy adjustments for study-abroad programs and assured the nation and the world that China would not reduce the number of its students and scholars going abroad (*China Education News*, 1986). As if Liu's explanations and assurances had not carried much weight, Li Peng, then Minister of the SEC, stated that "Sending people through various forms to study in foreign countries conforms entirely with our country's open policies and caters to the need of the Four Modernizations. It must be continued for a long time to come" (1986).

To dispel some new rumors a couple of years later, Huang Xinbai (1988), President of the Chinese Education Association for International Exchanges (CEAIE), stated that China's policy of sending students and scholars for advanced studies and research remained unchanged and would never change. His statement was again endorsed by Li Peng, who had become Premier of China, during his state visit to Australia. "China will continue to send students abroad and will do it in a better way" (1988). The validity of these statements and assurances were borne out by the statistics of the Chinese students and scholars going to the United States. According to the most authoritative study conducted in the United States, Chinese students and scholars had been going to the United States in increasing numbers over the past several years. In 1979, a total of 807 students and scholars on government and institutional programs went to the United States. In 1987, the number increased to 8179. The number of self-financed students expanded from 523 in 1979 to 5235 in 1987. Both categories of students and scholars showed a tenfold increase over a period of eight years, amid all the rumors of reduction (Orleans, 1988, p. 88). As of mid-1989, there were 43,000 Chinese students and scholars on American university campuses (Orleans, 1989).

The Brain Drain

By 1988, 22,000 Chinese students and scholars had returned upon completion of their studies and research in foreign countries, according to Yu Fuzeng, Director of the Foreign Affairs Bureau of the SEC (1988). This figure was supported by Orleans (1988), who estimated that a total of 19,500 Chinese students and scholars had returned to China from the United States alone by January 1988. Orleans further stated that through 1986, "almost all of China's government-sponsored and one-third of the self-sponsoring students and scholars who completed their studies returned home" (p. 43).

With their newly acquired knowledge and expertise, these returned students and scholars had been playing key roles in China's higher education, scientific research and production management. For example, of the 36 institutions of higher learning directly administered by the SEC, 17 were headed by returned scholars (Li, 1988). Besides taking up administrative responsibilities, many returned students and scholars had assumed leadership roles in their fields of study, making up 30 to 50 percent of all advisors of graduate courses. Some had been instrumental in establishing areas of study and research new to China (Yu).

The vital role of these returned students and scholars was further evidenced by reports from individual institutions of higher learning. Among the 96 returned scholars of Zhejiang University in the mid-1980s, 81 became advisors for master's and doctoral programs, and 36 assumed responsibilities of heads of teaching and research faculties or of directors of laboratories. Lu Yongxiang, who was appointed president of the university, had been a visiting scholar at a West German university from 1979 to 1981. After his return, he continued to distinguish himself in research. Among his four new inventions, one was patented in West Germany and the others in China. The academic achievements of the president and many other returned faculty members enabled Zhejiang University to become a first-rate university in China and a university with international recognition (Huang, 1987).

Similar contributions by returned students and scholars had been reported by other universities. At Qinghua, China's leading university of science and engineering, the 437 returned faculty members offered 385 new courses and undertook tens of new research projects (Zhang, 1988).

In short, China benefitted much from the study-abroad programs it had been aggressively pursuing over the ten years. These programs not only provided a catalyst for the rejuvenation of China's paralyzed higher education, but also trained and upgraded invaluable human resources for its future development.

But the gains were accompanied by losses or fears of losses. The "rising tide of going abroad" in the 1980s depleted a few research institutions of their bright young employees and placed some colleges and universities in an emergency situation in terms of faculty members. A newspaper report disclosed that one academic department at a Shanghai university had to suspend its enrollment because the majority of the faculty had gone overseas (Du, 1990). It was not uncommon for many national-echelon colleges and universities to have one-third of their faculty members working for advanced degrees at foreign universities.

Moreover, a growing number of Chinese students and scholars were extending their stays or trying to seek permanent residency in foreign countries. As many as 8500 Chinese students and scholars had managed to remain in the United States "either by legally changing their status or simply disappearing into the American melting pot" between 1978 and 1988 (Orleans, 1988, p. 9). Though the loss of their precious talent was not uncommon for developing countries, it was particularly damaging to China for very compelling reasons. First, China's ambitious Four Modernizations drive needed huge numbers of highly professional and skilled human resources, especially those trained in the industrialized West with knowledge and expertise in frontier disciplines. Second, no other country had sent so many of its intellectual assets to foreign countries in a matter of ten years. In fact, a whole new generation of China's potential leaders in all fields of learning was being educated in capitalist countries. Though China predicted that there would inevitably be some loss of talent in such extensive exchange programs, the rapidity and the extent with which the brain drain had been developing presented a challenge well beyond China's expectations.

The reasons for China's brain drain were political, professional and economic. It was true that since the late 1970s, China had stopped incessant class struggles and repressive political movements. It was also true that instead of being subjected to constant thought remolding as a class alien to the CCP and the nation's socialist cause, the intellectuals had come to be regarded as mental workers politically equal with workers and farmers. But suspicion of the intellectuals had not been thoroughly eradicated. During the 1980s, continual minor political campaigns were waged. In 1981, a screenplay *Bitter Love* was criticized nationwide. In 1983, the anticultural pollution movement was undertaken. In 1987, "bourgeois liberalization" was denounced. Though these political/ideological struggles were not as intense and oppressive as political movements before the 1980s, they were specifically directed against the decadent Western values and ideas to which the intellectuals were believed to be most susceptible. These movements, though well intentioned and for the good of China, were reminiscent of the horrors of the Cultural Revolution and often misconstrued. So the fears, though unfounded, constituted one of the reasons why some intellectuals left China and decided not to return.

Professional satisfaction was another factor that prompted Chinese students and scholars to extend their stay or to decide to remain permanently in the West. The comparatively up-to-date, adequate facilities and equipment for basic as well as applied research, the comparatively easy access to information and, above all, the relative freedom of expression, all of which were often nonexistent in China, understandably attracted highly capable, aspiring Chinese students and scholars.

Besides political and professional considerations, life-style and material comfort offered another enticement to some Chinese, particularly young, impressionable students. Compared with China, which had a per capita GNP of US$ 355 (*Asiaweek,* February 2, 1990, p. 6), the industrialized West was manifestly affluent. Both the living and working conditions were better and more congenial to academic development. However, the wealth and material comfort would not lure many Chinese students and scholars if intellectuals were reasonably remunerated in China. As already discussed, the income of many Chinese intellectuals relative to that of manual laborers had declined considerably in the 1980s. This inequity made many students hesitate to return, at least immediately upon completing their studies. Whether materialistic or not, some Chinese students declared openly that they would at least remain in the West long enough to earn and save money, claiming that without these savings, they might "starve" if and when they returned to China (Wang, 1989).

Whatever the reason, the nonreturn or delay in return of Chinese students and scholars distressed Chinese authorities, but precipitated few drastic actions or unhappy international incidents. Perhaps very little could be done about this problem. Once these Chinese students and scholars were overseas, there was no way to coerce them to return except to "create a climate for attracting and retaining talent" (Orleans, 1988, p. 55), which could not be easily accomplished. Aware of this dilemma, Chinese authorities seemed to have adopted a rather conciliatory attitude. Instead of issuing harsh statements or denouncing defections, the Chinese government reiterated that reasonable requests for extension should be considered under the circumstances prescribed by the regulations and laws of host countries (Li, 1988, and Yu, 1989). Even for those who had obtained permanent residency in the West, continued concern and solicitude should be extended (Yu, 1989).

This was seen to be a wise policy on the part of the Chinese government. From a long-term point of view, the brain drain would not be a complete loss for China. Delayed returns would enable Chinese students and scholars to acquire more practical experience in their fields of study, which China was not yet well equipped to provide. Also, given China's present level of scientific and technological development, it would be more profitable to have its talent continuously upgraded in the West than to have it back and then underused or even wasted. In this sense, the industrialized West could actually be utilized as a repository or a perpetual training ground of the precious scientific and professional personnel essential to China's future development (Wang, 1989).

The same rationale could be applied to those who had already emigrated to the West. Wherever they lived, these "offspring of the Yellow Emperor" would remain committed to their native land. This was evidenced by generous, significant contributions by millions of overseas Chinese living in many parts of the world who still "retain a strong sense of loyalty and obligation" to China (Maddox and Thurston, 1987). Many of them had been acting as a "major, distinct constituency" in promoting China's extensive scholarly and academic exchanges with foreign countries (Maddox and Thurston). Some had spent substantial amounts of time or money for the sake of China's scientific and educational development. The deeply ingrained patriotic sentiments and Confucian tradition made it possible for the Chinese in all parts of the world to transcend political differences to contribute to the prosperity of the Chinese nation. "Every one of us is proud of being Chinese. We won't forget our roots and will do everything we can for our motherland," said a distinguished American political scientist of Chinese descent (Chang, 1989). With the older generation of overseas Chinese setting the example, there was every reason to believe that the younger generation would not turn their backs on their motherland. Disillusionment with a political party was temporary, but the love they cherished for the nation and their eagerness to contribute to its development were everlasting.

The "reverse flow" of students and scholars from Taiwan in recent years might also be evidence that the brain drain would only be temporary and, therefore, should not be a big worry for China. From the 1950s through the 1960s, only about 10 percent of students from Taiwan studying in foreign countries went back each year upon completion of their studies. But since the early 1980s, the return rate had steadily increased to 40 percent. The major reasons for the increasing return rate were the economic revitalization, rising standards of living and, more significantly, the growing political democratization. If China could sustain the momentum of its political and economic reforms and significantly improve the living and working conditions for intellectuals, it would eventually have little difficulty attracting most, if not all, of its talented people back (*Chinese Youth News*, January 30, 1989, p. 3).

So if Chinese authorities could rationalize that the extension of stay or nonreturn of their students and scholars was temporary and that certain advantages might accrue to China from these extended or permanent overseas sojourns, the brain drain issue would "lose some of its immediate gravity" (Orleans, 1988, p. 56). From a long-term, strategic point of view, "China's loss of a certain proportion of students should be neither a 'complete loss' nor a national crisis" (Orleans, p. 121).

In spite of this possible rationalization, it was painful and embarrassing for the Chinese to have so many of the nation's gifted youth and valuable scholars opting to stay in other countries. So the Chinese government had been appealing to the patriotic sentiments of its students and scholars. It reiterated that while modern science and technology might transcend national boundaries, scientists and professional people belonged to different nations, and those who were studying abroad, especially those funded by the government, were obligated to return and serve China. In addition to the patriotic appeals, Chinese authorities decided to send more scholars for shorter visits, emphasized the close links between China's needs and the choice of programs and extended a variety of favors to returned students and scholars (Sun, 1989).

The United States and Chinese Students and Scholars

With their autonomy, flexibility and resilience, American institutions of higher learning attracted and accepted more Chinese students and scholars than any other country in the world. Since the normalization of Sino-U.S. relations, Chinese students and scholars had been going to the United States in such numbers and by such a variety of means that their exact statistics had eluded both American and Chinese computations. Orleans, a long-time China specialist, lamented that "Neither the Chinese nor the Americans know precisely how many Chinese students and scholars are in the United States now or at any time since the exchanges began in 1978" (1988, Preface).

Although the exact statistics were unavailable, it was reported that American colleges and universities spent US$ 200 million a year in supporting Chinese students and scholars in the United States (Shive, 1990). One could not help but ask if this financial support was appropriated without any self-interest.

It was true that China had much to learn from advanced U.S. science and technology and was, therefore, the primary beneficiary of the extensive scholarly and academic exchanges they had been eagerly pursuing with the United States. But the United States benefitted from these exchanges as well. It was a giver of favors as well as a recipient of benefits. Although the United States had few national policies regarding the education and training of foreign students in general or Chinese students and scholars in particular (Maddox and Thurston), a number of discernible motivations prompted and sustained these exchanges. As early as 1981, Clough summarized ten major factors behind the willingness and enthusiasm of the United States to support exchanges with China. Among the ten motivating factors identified, some were altruistic: the Americans were eager to "provide scientific gains in certain areas" to "contribute to the development of a 'strong, secure, and peaceful China'" (p. 7). But some were egoistic as well. While contributing to the economic strength and prosperity of China, the United States could more easily compete in an expanding commercial market. Moreover, it was strategically crucial for the United States to "establish important contacts with the younger generation of Chinese scientists and engineers, who will likely furnish much of the future leadership of China" (p. 7).

This last strategic objective was underscored by an American physicist. Speaking of America's opportunity to influence thousands of Chinese students and scholars, the physicist stated that "an understanding of the unique way in which scientific research is organized and pursued in the United States is even more important than the transfer of scientific knowledge itself" (Clough, p. 61). An American diplomat put it even more bluntly by suggesting that the United States would be much "worse off" if the future leaders of China were educated in the Soviet Union or Japan (Clough, p. 61).

On the more practical side, U.S. universities were eager to attract the "largest pool of untapped talent" from China. Maddox and Thurston (1987) claimed that the top physics students on many American university campuses were invariably Chinese, in spite of language difficulties. This claim was supported by Orleans, who stated that the Chinese students and scholars had made a "very positive impression" and were "an especially valuable addition to the U.S. academic community" (1988, p. 118). Competitive, intelligent and hard-working, many Chinese students became indispensable teaching and research assistants to American academics, particularly those in science and engineering. In engineering, where there was a serious shortage of U.S.

graduate students, the Chinese filled a "recognized need" (Orleans, 1988, p. 118).

Of course, Chinese authorities were well aware of the quality of their students and scholars studying or working overseas and of the danger of "contaminations" by American values and ideas. Although they appreciated the opportunities American institutions of higher learning had been able and willing to provide for their students and scholars, they were displeased with the relative ease with which their students and scholars could manage or managed to circumvent the U.S. immigration laws for extended or permanent stays. "China's brain-drain problem would be insignificant were it not for the United States" (Orleans, 1988 p. 38).

According to official Chinese estimates, about 10 percent of the government-funded students had not returned upon completing their studies. Among the 20,000 self-financing students, only several hundred had returned. For most Chinese institutions of higher learning, the 10 percent nonreturnees had gone to the United States. The majority of the self-funded students were also studying at American colleges and universities or had managed to change their student status and had integrated into American society.

In spite of the loss of talent, Chinese authorities did not stop or reduce the numbers of their students and scholars to the United States, as the gains from the exchanges far outweighed the losses in long-term, strategic considerations. For the Americans, the cost was an investment in a worthy cause. As both sides would gain in the final analysis, the challenge was how best to maintain this delicate balance and prevent incidents which might "kill the goose that lays the golden eggs."

The Utilization of Returned Students and Scholars

In addition to the brain-drain dilemma, Chinese authorities had to solve the problem of utilizing their returned students and scholars. If they could not prevent the brain drain, they were capable of utilizing the talent of those who had begun coming back in significant numbers since the early 1980s.

By an official account, 70 percent of the 14,000 returnees by 1984 were not being "fully used because of a shortage of advanced facilities and unsuitable work assignments" (*China Daily,* November 30, 1984, p. 5). In addition, funds for scientific research were inadequate and research assistants were not available. Perhaps more frustrating than these practical difficulties was the inefficiency of the entrenched and unsympathetic bureaucrats, who were untutored in science but nevertheless issuing orders. Also, some returned students were resentful of their older colleagues, who had most of the priorities for academic promotion and for research grants on the basis of seniority. With the limitation of the quotas for advanced academic rank and the scarcity of research funds, young scholars had to wait for years before they could expect to make a name for themselves. These problems were compounded by difficulties in reassimilation after years of relatively congenial working environments and comfortable life styles in developed Western countries.

To alleviate these problems and help returned students and scholars to fully utilize their knowledge and expertise, Chinese authorities had developed a number of measures that proved to be effective. To begin with, opportunities for job choice were being increased. Instead of arbitrarily assigning jobs to these returned students as it did with most of the home-trained students, the government allowed the returned students a choice of working in government organizations, for Sino-foreign joint ventures or for enterprises under collective ownership. Returned students were also allowed to run enterprises or companies with self-raised funds. To assist the returning students in their choice, the government had established the Chinese Returned Students Service Center to provide links between the potential employers and the students. By late 1988, the center had helped 109 students with advanced, foreign degrees to secure suitable positions. Due to its outstanding service, the center was receiving dozens of letters from overseas per month inquiring about possible job vacancies in China (Wei, 1989).

To aid the returned PhD recipients who failed to find a satisfactory position, the government had established 145 postdoctoral research stations, which covered 21 branches of science and were located in 89 universities or research institutes. These temporary holding places accommodated about 40 percent of all returned students with PhD's from foreign universities (Wei, 1989). Subject to approval, the returned PhD recipients could choose to work at any of these postdoctoral stations for a period of two years and receive a substantial grant for their research projects. Twenty-five percent of the grants could be used to supplement living costs in addition to generous living allowances provided by the government. Over recent years, the State Planning Commission in Beijing made special appropriations to construct apartment buildings for these postdoctoral researchers. Many blocks had already been completed (Yu, 1989).

Besides improving the job-assignment system and providing preferential working and living conditions for returned students, the government had made other special provisions. When returned students and scholars could not continue their highly sophisticated research in China due to the lack of facilities, they were permitted to work alternately at home and abroad, conducting their work overseas while establishing their discipline at home. In addition, young scholars on government programs could apply to go overseas again when they fulfilled their terms of service in China (Wei). If, after all the efforts, young returned students still could not find a job commensurate with their training, they would be sent to study or work at foreign institutions again by the government (Yu).

To promote distinguished returned students and scholars to the senior academic rank, the government made plans to balance the number of returned students accepted by research institutes and universities with the quotas of senior academic titles for these institutions. This meant that these returned students and scholars would be promoted to appropriate senior academic ranks on the basis of merit without the constraint of quota limitations. Many returned PhD recipients had actually skipped grades and been appointed full professors. "Individuals returning from experiences overseas have tended to advance more rapidly within administrative and research establishments" in China (Reed, 1988, p. 102).

Although the government had been extending many favors to the returning students, unrealistic expectations that resulted from a long sojourn in the relatively affluent West often led to frustrations and estrangement. Reintegration into the domestic environment and a satisfactory professional career for the returned students and scholars depended, to a considerable extent, upon their adequate understanding of China's present level of economic development and upon a balanced judgment of their own worth and abilities. Thus, it was perhaps necessary for the returned students to ask what they could do for their country before they made demands on the government.

The Fifth Modernization?

In sending its students and scholars to the capitalist West, China ran two major risks: the brain drain, which was discussed as inevitable, and the adverse impact of Western ideas and values, which was likewise unavoidable.

To minimize the impact, Chinese authorities had adopted countermeasures, such as the movements against cultural pollution and against bourgeois liberalization. The CCP strengthened its political/ideological work among the intellectuals to constantly reinforce orthodox, Communist ideas and ideals. And to resist Western influences in its modernization process, China had been insisting on the Four Cardinal Principles for building socialism with Chinese characteristics. Parallel with the socialism with Chinese characteristics, China also claimed to be establishing a higher education system with Chinese features. This meant that instead of indiscriminately adopting foreign patterns, China would adapt Western science, technology and managerial experience according to specific Chinese conditions. Modernization should not and would not, lead to Westernization.

But these objectives were not easy to attain. In the age of technology and information, it was increasingly difficult to abandon the ideological package wrapped in modern science and technology. As one China expert commented:

> Returned scholars have brought home with them not only knowledge of computers and plasma physics, but also a whole range of administrative, management and institutional forms that in their minds are closely associated with the knowledge thus obtained. [Hawkins, 1984]

The growing demand in China for freedom and democracy and the outbreak of the massive student demonstrations in December 1986 and January 1987 fully testified to this problem. In China's Four Modernizations, persistent voices for one more modernization—the democratization of the system—had been loud and clear. One newspaper article, for example, implored that since China had no problems introducing modern science, technology and management techniques from the West, it should not refuse to introduce and absorb new ideologies, concepts and methodologies, which were intricately linked with the development of the industrialized nations (Yang, 1986). The possibility of the fifth modernization was heightened by people in the West, who, consciously or unconsciously, pressed their own values on visiting Chinese students and scholars with the hope that the Chinese students and scholars would "create pressure on the government to change" upon their return (Maddox and Thurston, p. 145).

It was obvious that China would not adopt all aspects of Western administrative, management systems or institutional forms. But how effectively it could absorb the suitable while discarding the unsuitable or, in short, how successfully it could modernize but not Westernize, presented a challenge, which would remain constant and challenging.

Summary

Sending students and scholars for studies and training at foreign universities was an integral, predominant part of China's scholarly and academic exchanges with other countries. Between 1978 and 1988, over 60,000 students and scholars were sent to 76 countries and regions. In addition, over 20,000 students went abroad to study at their own expense. The majority of these students and scholars had studied or were still studying in the United States.

With the changing needs and circumstances of China over the past decade, there had been frequent policy modifications with respect to these extensive study-abroad programs. For example, adjustments were made as to the type of people to be selected and sent for advanced studies or training overseas, and some specific policies fluctuated for students applying to study abroad at their own expense. In spite of these modifications, China did not alter its overall policy of sending students and scholars to other countries, particularly to the industrialized West. Under this general policy, China had been sending a steadily increasing number of students and scholars for study-abroad programs.

In sending huge numbers of its best and brightest to the capitalist West, Chinese authorities had three major concerns: 1) what percentage of the students and scholars would return upon completion of their studies; 2) how China could best utilize the newly acquired knowledge and expertise of its returned students and scholars and 3) what influence these returned students and scholars might have on Chinese society.

These were legitimate concerns. While most students and scholars on government and institutional programs had returned upon completion of their studies, a few decided to stay behind. And the majority of the self-financed students would most likely be lost to the industrialized West, especially to the United States. This brain drain would naturally affect China's educational and scientific development and distress Chinese authorities. But viewed from a long-term, strategic perspective, the nonreturn of a proportion of students and scholars would not be a complete loss or a national crisis. Considering the present level of China's scientific and economic development and the strong patriotic sentiments of the Chinese wherever they live, China would perhaps eventually gain from these temporary, expected losses.

To address the second concern, Chinese authorities had taken a variety of measures ranging from improving job assignments to providing favorable working and living conditions. Provisions had also been made to promote returned students and scholars to advanced academic positions. By any standards, these favors appeared to be substantial and attractive.

The key role these returned students and scholars had been playing justified the favors. With new, advanced knowledge and expertise they had developed in the industrialized West, these students and scholars were indispensable to China's education, science and technology, and many became and would become leaders in their fields. But these people had returned with not only enhanced professional knowledge and skills, but also some Western values and ideas. This "double-edged sword" presented potential threats to Chinese authorities who were eager to modernize, but not to Westernize China.

7

Into the 1990s and the Twenty-first Century

The ten years between 1978 and 1988 are characterized as a decade of China's dramatic socioeconomic reforms and of open-door policies. It is regarded as a decade with the most sustained "domestic tranquility that China has experienced in a century" and as a decade with a pace and extent of change unparalleled in China's entire history (Oksenberg, 1989). Under these favorable circumstances, Chinese higher education has undergone unprecedented reforms and made notable achievements. By building on existing strengths and adapting pertinent foreign patterns and practices, a new, distinctly Chinese system of higher education has begun to take shape slowly but steadily.

After ten years of notable initiatives and marked achievements, how will China's higher education develop in the remaining years of the twentieth century and beyond? The answer to this question should be not only a logical closing chapter of this study, but also a necessary, meaningful attempt for two compelling reasons.

First, the development of Chinese higher education has reached a kind of plateau following the ten years of dramatic change. How the momentum of the reform can be maintained is critical to the establishment of a steadily improving system of higher education in China. Second, in a relatively authoritarian, centralized political and economic system, educational development is, to a greater degree than in other systems, either facilitated or constrained by the turn of events in economic and political spheres. Chinese higher education has been, in fact, developing within a social milieu that is itself in the process of dramatic change. Beginning in the late 1980s, China has been experiencing a significant readjustment in its economic and political reforms. How well its higher education can survive the readjustment and its consequent austerity measures has, therefore, become an overriding concern.

To predict the future development of Chinese higher education, it is necessary to bear in mind China's specific conditions. China is a developing country with 1.1 billion people. At the present rate of increase, the country's population will reach 1.3 billion by the end of the twentieth century (Hou, 1990). Of the current 1.1 billion people, 268 million or 23.5 percent are illiterates or semiilliterates (*People's Daily,* Overseas Edition, May 7, 1990, p. 1), and about 75 percent live in rural areas, engaging in mostly manual labor to produce, on 7 percent of the world's arable land, enough grain to feed approximately 22 percent of the world's population (Hou, 1990). As a result, China's per capita gross national product at present only amounts to US$ 355 (*Asiaweek,* February 2, 1990, p. 6). With the rapid modernization of its agriculture, industry and science and technology, China aims at increasing, before the end of the twentieth century, its per capita GNP to between US$ 800 and 1000 and its per capita grain output to about 400 kilograms. When this goal is reached, China will be relatively prosperous.

What all these statistics mean to China's education in general and higher education in particular is that educational investment has been and may remain insufficient. Over the years, the government's appropriations for education have been fluctuating between 2 and 3 percent of the GNP or 10 percent of the total government expenditures (Han and Wu, 1989; Liu, 1989). The per capita education spending amounted to US$ 8 in the early and middle 1980s, less than one-sixtieth of the spending in Japan and one-hundredth of the spending in the United States (Xu, 1989). According to China's State Statistics Bureau (1989), China's educational expenses in proportion to gross national product ranked one hundredth in the world, and its per capita educational expenses came to about 25 percent that of the developing countries.

These statistics also signify a formidable challenge to Chinese education. If China is to be transformed from a relatively poor, backward and agrarian economy into a fairly prosperous, advanced and industrial economy, the whole nation has to be, first of all, adequately educated. But with the staggering numbers of illiterates and semiilliterates and an average of less than five years of education per person (Li, 1989), China's modernization process would naturally be seriously handicapped.

In view of China's specific situation and the problems that are inherent in its higher education or that have been exacerbated in the reform process, the following scenarios are deemed possible in the development of Chinese higher education during the remaining years of the twentieth century and beyond.

Scenarios

Education Outlay

Judging from the present level of economic development and the austerity measures that have been adopted, the government appropriations for education may not likely register a substantial increase. Over the years, there has been considerable rhetoric regarding education as key to the survival and prosperity of the Chinese nation. There has also been the promise of an increase in the education budget. In fact, funding for education has been growing at an average annual rate of 15 percent. But the double-digit inflation has offset the increase and, worse still, brought about an actual drop in education outlay (*China Daily*, April 6, 1989, p. 4). With the present stringent measures to curb inflation, the recentralizing effort to streamline and revitalize economic development and the pressure of many social groups, education expenditures may increase by 1 percent of the GNP or reach 15 percent of the total government spending. If higher education continues to receive 20 percent of the total amount of educational funding, this limited increase may not provide higher education with sufficient operating budgets. The insufficiency will likely compel colleges and universities to continue seeking alternative sources of funding.

Institutions and Enrollment

Restrained by the low level of government appropriations and determined by the needs of China's present economic development, the number of traditional institutions of higher learning will not increase in the near future and the enrollment at these institutions will level off. One of the primary aims in reforming higher education is to ensure its stable and proportionate development for better service to the nation. With 1075 traditional institutions of higher learning and about 1400 adult institutions, China has already had a total of 4 million college students. In proportion with the nation's population, this is by no means a significant number. But according to predictions by Chinese authorities, it is, for the time being, sufficient for China's need for high-level intellectual manpower (Li, 1989).

While Chinese higher education remains at its present level, the emphasis of reform will be placed on improving the quality of colleges and universities and adjusting their structure, levels and curricula to better serve China's socioeconomic development. In fact, with the ongoing effort to streamline the 200 institutions of higher learning that were hastily established during the mid-1980s, the total number of the traditional institutions of higher learning may be somewhat reduced as a result of the subsequent amalgamation of overlapping colleges and the downgrading of substandard colleges. The reduction will help raise the efficiency of management and improve the quality of instruction.

"Multilevels, Multiforms and Multistandards"

Of the present 1075 traditional institutions of higher learning, about two-thirds are administered by provincial, municipal or prefectural authorities (Liu, 1987). The rest are managed by either the SEC or other central government commissions and ministries. In the Chinese system of higher education, the level of management signifies the level of hierarchy and the concomitant prestige and concentration of resources, both human and material.

In the years to come, traditional institutions of higher learning may continue to be classified into three distinct levels. The bottom level will consist of the majority of the local institutions including the 345 colleges with short-cycle, specialized technical programs and many three-year teacher-training colleges (Yang, 1990). Oriented to local needs and services, these institutions will mainly focus on teaching. Limited research may be undertaken, but it will largely be geared to local economic development. Students will continue to be drawn locally, and the graduates will likewise be absorbed by the locality.

Above these market-driven, teaching-oriented institutions are many fairly well established four-year colleges and universities with relatively adequate library holdings, laboratory facilities and qualified and experienced faculty members. While continuing to concentrate on teaching at the baccalaureate level, these institutions may offer limited numbers of graduate programs and undertake certain numbers of research projects.

At the top of the hierarchy may again be the key institutions with priority in the allocation of resources and the opportunities for international exchanges. These colleges and universities will become "the two centers": the center of teaching and the center of research (Zhu, 1988). Many may have graduate schools.

So Chinese institutions of higher learning will, for a long time to come, form the clear shape of a pyramid with the apex being a few key, national institutions and the base being the vast majority of the nonkey, local colleges. The middle part will consist mainly of many provincial-level colleges and universities with teaching as the major focus. What this pyramidal shape holds for the future of China's higher education is a more pronounced stratification in status, responsibility and standard.

At present, the hierarchy favors the top-echelon institutions. Those which are under central authorities are in a more advantageous position than locally administered institutions with regard to student enrollment, faculty recruitment, curriculum design, fund allocation and scholarly exchanges with foreign countries. Most reform initiatives have in fact originated and emanated from these leading academic establishments and may continue to do so. Their susceptibility to the change in the nation's political climate is not likely to diminish their ability to act as pacesetters in academic standards.

The vast majority of the colleges and universities may continue to follow the pace and standard set by the few bellwethers. But in a fast diversifying economy, this uniformity will have to be broken. It might be predicted then that pacesetting, key institutions will emerge at the lower levels and for different types of institutions. This will enable the Chinese to build up new-style, dynamic tertiary institutions which may be second or third echelon but do not provide merely a watered-down university curriculum. Fostering key, exemplary institutions for all levels and types of colleges and universities will naturally take time. But to invigorate Chinese higher education and to make it more efficient in the nation's service, it is inevitable and imperative for these institutions to emerge.

In addition to the sustained hierarchical development with accompanying diversity of responsibilities and standards, Chinese higher education may witness further diversity in form. If traditional institutions are not to increase in number and in enrollment to conform to the nation's economic development, the future growth in the number of institutions and in enrollment is expected to take place in the nontraditional sector. This is due to the comparatively low cost of running these institutions and, more significantly, to the market-oriented courses offered by these institutions. For example, over 90 percent of the programs are and may continue to be vocational and technical, thus filling a significant need for middle-level manpower in China's modernization process.

As Chinese institutions of higher learning, both traditional and nontraditional, develop toward many levels, forms and standards, their names may continue to be as confusing as ever. To begin with, colleges (or institutes), which are limited in course offerings, and universities, which consist of liberal arts and sciences or of technical programs, will continue to have equal status. A college may have vigorous, first-rate academic programs at both undergraduate and graduate levels and is, therefore, no less prestigious than a well-established university. Chinese universities are not truly comprehensive in their academic programs. Though there is a noticeable trend toward a broadening of programs embracing engineering, sciences, liberal arts, law and business, Chinese universities have a long way to go to achieve a comprehensiveness in the Western sense of the term. Only a few universities at the pinnacle of the hierarchy can claim to be moving toward and eventually reaching that goal.

To add to the confusion, many of the rapidly emerging community colleges and adult institutions often have the glamorous name of "university." The name becomes more misleading when such an institution bears the name of the big city where it is located, Guangzhou (Canton) University and Xi'an University, for example.

Perhaps little may or could be done about the names. After all, this is not a vital issue. What is more significant is that a concerted, sustained effort is being made toward a healthy, increasing diversification of the higher education system for China's avowed modernization goals.

Modes of Development

How, then, will the diversification be maintained and expanded? To answer this question, it is necessary to bear in mind that China is a developing country with limited material resources and intellectual manpower and with a considerable degree of economic and cultural disparity among its different regions. Moreover, the increasing market regulation in the nation's economic development has led to a decentralization in all spheres of Chinese life. In higher education, local authorities have gained more power in supervising institutions of higher learning in their localities, and colleges and universities themselves have begun to enjoy a degree of autonomy in management never known before.

So Chinese higher education may experience a kind of "rolling" development, which means that the coastal areas, with their comparatively advanced economy, science and culture, will set an example for and assist in the development of higher education in the hinterland and national minority regions. This mode of regional cooperation has actually begun, with many colleges and universities in the big cities such as Shanghai and Beijing sending their faculty members in rotation to help with the programs of the newly established colleges and universities in Xinjiang, Tibet, Guizhou and a number of other provinces or national minority regions. For a balanced economic and educational development in China, this kind of cooperation will be undertaken in a more organized, mutually beneficial way in the years to come.

In addition, Chinese higher education may develop in a "radial" manner. China's institutions of higher learning are concentrated in a few densely populated cities which are also the nation's key political, economic and cultural centers, cities such as Beijing, Shanghai, Xi'an, Nanjing, Wuhan, Chengdu and Chongqing. The concentrated intellectual manpower and facilities will spread to and benefit the surrounding areas of these big centers, like spokes from a hub.

These modes of development are likely to be expedited by the expanded power of provincial-level education commissions to supervise and coordinate the programs of the colleges and universities in their localities in spite of the different affiliations of these institutions. The "rolling" and "radiating" modes of development may also be promoted by the greater autonomy which institutions of higher learning have gained in management and curriculum design. With less intervention from central authorities and less administrative red tape, institutions of higher learning and local governments and enterprises may find it easier to increase, on the basis of mutual benefit, the partnership relations that have already begun to be established.

Internationalization

Along with increase in regional cooperation, Chinese higher education will become more international in character. As collaboration among different types and levels of colleges and universities and between higher education and society in China increases, interaction in higher education among the world's major countries will also grow.

Chinese higher education will become more international in character because it has been extensively borrowing from and absorbing foreign practices and patterns over the past decade. Over the years, China has learned, the hard way, that science is quintessentially universal, transcending national boundaries. "The desire to enclose oneself within artificial barriers is, first of all, to condemn oneself to stagnation and, secondly, to regression" (Lavroff, 1985). It is impossible for one nation to develop a higher education system on purely national knowledge and experience. It is also impossible to identify a nation with an educational system not influenced one way or another by the ideas and patterns of other nations.

Another reason Chinese higher education will become more international is that countries in the world are growing more interdependent, and many professions are being internationalized. Any system of higher education is thus compelled to be more international so that it will be able to better prepare professionals to function in a widening range of fields on a global basis.

The internationalization of Chinese higher education may continue to be promoted by the nation's unprecedented effort in international exchange programs since the late 1970s. This international educational interaction has not abated despite the recent setback in China's relations with a few major world powers, as evidenced by the fact that arrival rates of Chinese students and scholars in the United States for the fall semester of 1989, according to a 1990 American IIE study, did not vary significantly from previous years. Neither did the fields of study and the academic level fluctuate (Strevy, Executive Summary).

While China continues to send students and scholars for advanced studies and research overseas, it will periodically modify specific policies governing study-abroad programs. For example, it will redirect the flow of students and scholars and adopt measures to increase profit from the extensive exchange programs. Reducing the scope of the exchanges already in progress would insulate China again from the world community and slow down China's modernization process. It may also worsen the relationship between the CCP and China's intellectuals, whose service is indispensable to the nation's socioeconomic development. Whether conservative or liberal, the Chinese leaders cannot afford to risk cutting China's international academic and scholarly exchanges. And nobody can reverse the trend of a broad international cooperation in an increasing number of fields in the age of information and technology.

In fact, the present Chinese leadership has repeatedly reassured the nation that the policies governing international exchanges in education will remain unchanged. The new CCP General Secretary, who studied abroad himself, has stressed that sending students and scholars overseas for advanced studies and research constitutes an integral part of China's reform efforts and opening policies (Jiang, 1990). As China continues to commit itself to reform and international cooperation, it will at least maintain the present scope of its international exchange programs.

Intensifying the CCP Leadership and Political/Ideological Work

While continuing to promote international exchanges in higher education, Chinese authorities are fully aware that Western values and ideas can undermine the CCP legitimacy and damage the building of an avowed Chinese-style socialism. For the past few years, there has been a persistent struggle against "bourgeois liberalization," which is believed to have resulted from cultural and educational exchanges with Western countries. In the wake of massive student unrest, the struggle has intensified.

The intensified struggle and the subsequent education in Marxist orthodoxy call for a strengthening of the CCP leadership in university management, which has already taken place. For example, it has been announced that the "president responsibility system" will not extend beyond the 103 colleges and universities. Instead, the CCP must strengthen its leading, nuclear position in all college and university affairs as a fundamental guarantee for the correct orientation of Chinese higher education (*People's Daily,* Overseas Edition, April, 13, 1990, p. 1).

Among the university students, education in patriotism, modern Chinese history and China's specific conditions is made compulsory. To facilitate the political/ideological work, faculty members, many of whom are members of the CCP, are exhorted to keep aware of their political responsibility, to play an exemplary role and to guide the students toward a correct political direction (*China Daily,* April 4, 1990, p. 3).

The intensified CCP control over colleges and universities and the political/ideological work among the students will continue because of China's established orthodoxy and its avowed socialist system. Higher education leads to professional as well as liberalized people and, as such, plays dual, conflicting roles: servant as well as critic of society. It is the conscience of society in addition to providing the society with much-needed intellectual manpower for economic development. The dual functions make higher education susceptible to various forms of governmental intervention and control, which are facilitated in China by the relatively high degree of centralized management in all spheres of life. Therefore, for political expediency, power can be delegated or retrieved, and the CCP control can be, at any time, loosened or tightened. As China moves into the twenty-first century, the CCP control and its concurrent political and ideological work will remain highly necessary and constant.

Scenarios (Summarized)

Considering China's specific circumstances—large population and low level of economic development—and the present scope of its higher education, the following scenarios seem to be possible during the decades ahead:

1) Education appropriations by the government may not experience a significant rise. While depending on the government for the bulk of their operating expenses, colleges and universities are likely to continue to seek diversified sources of funding.

2) No new traditional colleges and universities will be established in the near future, and the total enrollment may stabilize. With no increase in the number of institutions and enrollment, the reform initiatives will focus on raising quality and improving structure.

3) The current effort to diversify and restructure higher education will be sustained in order to make higher education better serve the nation's modernization drive. Nontraditional postsecondary education which trains much-needed but highly insufficient middle-level technical and vocational personnel may therefore be expanded significantly. The three-tiered administrative hierarchy will continue with concomitant differences in status and responsibilities.

4) Chinese higher education may "roll" from coastal to inland areas and "radiate" from key cities to surrounding regions. With the central-level State Education Commission exercising macromanagement, local educational administrations will have more power in promoting these modes of development and in coordinating the programs of the colleges and universities in their localities.

Recommendations

To ensure and promote the sustained, continuous reforms and achievements of Chinese higher education, the following recommendations are made for the development of Chinese higher education during the decades ahead.

Legislation

As it evolved, Chinese higher education followed a tortuous path characterized by efforts against the internal laws on education and by indiscriminate borrowing of foreign patterns, both resulting in serious setbacks. The major cause of the setbacks appears, in the final analysis, to be the lack of legislation and consistent policies governing major aspects of higher education development. Often, policies have been formulated for political expediencies or even at personal whims. And lack of proper supervision has caused good decrees to be consciously or unconsciously misinterpreted and carried to excesses. Worse still, countermeasures have been occasionally contrived for unjustifiable reasons. The unstable policies and their inconsistent implementation have made Chinese higher education a victim for party politics, as at the time of the Cultural Revolution. Without a stable, coercive and comprehensive law guaranteeing the rights and obligations of higher education, its effective, sustained development has been frequently impeded.

It is therefore recommended that an Education Law be drawn up and enforced. This should be a comprehensive, basic law, setting down the principles, tasks and systems of Chinese education. Its fundamental function would be to give concrete expression to the principles of education laid down in the Constitution of the PRC and to provide a basis for formulating and executing other pieces of education legislation.

With the basic Education Law formulated and enacted, it is recommended that a Teachers' Law and an Education Investment Law be drawn up and promulgated. The Teachers' Law should stipulate the qualifications, evaluations, rewards, penalties, rights and obligations of teachers at different levels of schools. The Investment Law should prescribe, in unequivocal terms, a fixed percentage of GNP designated for the use of education relative to the nation's economic growth. Other stipulations should be prescribed to help institutions of higher learning obtain funds from alternative sources and to prevent the kind of misappropriation or misuse of funds which have been not uncommon occurrences over the past ten years.

These and other laws, deliberated, formulated and enforced, will ensure education, especially higher education, *legalis homo* and make it less vulnerable to China's political expediencies. The laws governing major aspects of education should also provide preconditions for the other recommendations that are to follow.

Investment and Management

Education is investment in human capital. It is a productive rather than a consumptive undertaking, as it is perceived by many Chinese. But until recent years, the importance of education has not been fully recognized in China. This lack of understanding is reflected in China's education investment, which has been low relative to that of other developing countries and relative to other Chinese government expenditures. Therefore, in addition to securing, by means of legislation, the basic level of government investment which should continue to make up the bulk of the funding for education, it is recommended that the rate of increase in educational appropriations exceed the rate of increase in the nation's economic growth, instead of the reverse, which has been the case for the past decade.

In addition to the continued increase in government appropriations, it is also recommended that a more diversified source of funding be explored, including education tax, remunerations from contracted teaching, research and social service, tuition and fees and donations from enterprises and individuals.

Although increasing government education outlays and diversifying the alternative sources of funding will provide necessary financial resources, money alone is not a panacea for all the problems facing Chinese higher education. For this reason, it is also recommended that the following measures be taken to raise the efficiency of Chinese higher education.

To begin with, the low teacher-student ratio should be improved. The SEC has mandated an average teacher-student ratio of 1:8 by the year 1990, which represents a significant increase from the current ratio of 1:5. But it is still far below that in other countries: for example, Japan (1:12), the USSR (1:15) and the United States (1:17) (Han and Wu, 1989).

There are several factors that contribute to this serious disproportion, but the once-hired, never-fired system of employment, or the "Iron Rice Bowl" practice, is the major reason. Many senior faculty members, by virtue of their seniority and their authority over their younger peers partly due to the inbreeding in the faculty composition, seldom or never do much classroom teaching. Additionally, many newly recruited faculty members do not assume much teaching responsibility because of the lack of experience.

To remedy this situation, it is recommended that the teachers undertake fixed, required numbers of hours of classroom teaching each week. If they are unable to teach either because of old age or lack of experience, they should be retired or should not be hired in the first place. In addition, graduate students should be entrusted with teaching responsibilities as part of their programs. With this experience, they should be able to begin teaching as soon as they are appointed to teaching positions.

Along with improving the teacher-student ratio, which should reduce cost but increase efficiency, steps should be taken to enlarge Chinese colleges and universities, increasing the current average enrollment of 1800. According to the World Bank study of Chinese higher education, there are substantial savings in unit recurrent cost in colleges and universities larger than the average size of 4000 to 5000. Unit recurrent cost generally declines or at least remains constant after a higher level of enrollment is reached in the range of 8000 to 10,000 (1986).

But as of 1988, only 39 colleges and universities had more than 5000 students, and over 800 colleges had fewer than 3000 students (Li, 1988). As the number of institutions of higher learning will not increase in the foreseeable future (Li, 1988), China should take measures to improve teaching and living conditions at its colleges and universities so that more students can be enrolled. Given the low teacher-student ratio, the increase in the number of students should be both necessary and possible.

Another strategy to raise efficiency is to reform the support-service system. Chinese colleges and universities are, as a rule, encumbered with a disproportionately large support staff responsible for physical plants including residences for faculty, staff and students, medical and catering services and primary and secondary schools for children of faculty and staff. With all these subsidiary services, Chinese colleges and universities are self-contained establishments, like minisocieties. To cut the expenses for this cumbersome structure, it is recommended that these support services be contracted to other social organizations as much as possible.

Research on Higher Education

The low efficiency and many of the other problems that Chinese higher education has experienced are due, in part, to insufficient research into the internal laws that govern higher education and into the external factors that influence its development. There has not been in China, for instance, systematic research on its higher education comparable to the comprehensive, thorough study undertaken in the United States by the Carnegie Commission, with more than 60 volumes of published reports. Due to the neglect of study on higher education and the consequent defects in management, marked rises and declines have been common in the development of Chinese higher education.

For example, of the present 1075 traditional institutions of higher learning, 477, or 44 percent, have been founded since 1978. From 1981 to 1985, the number of colleges and universities increased from 675 to 1016, at an average annual rate of 68. In 1985 alone, 114 new colleges emerged (Liu, 1987). This rate of increase, reminiscent of the unchecked expansion of higher education during the impetuous years of the Great Leap Forward (1958-1959), is too fast to be advantageous. Realizing the potential danger of such a sudden, sharp rise, the SEC had to recall the already delegated accreditation authority from provincial-level education departments, hastily draw up the regulation with respect to the establishment of new institutions of higher learning and mandate decrees to streamline the 200-some colleges which did not meet the required standards.

To avoid similar faults and promote the development of higher education on a sound basis, it is recommended that the SEC organize task forces consisting of educational leaders, experts and representatives from all professions. The mission of these task forces would be to look into such issues as education and the nation's socioeconomic development, faculty and student concerns, effective educational leadership in a climate of change, rational and viable structure, curriculum design and development, higher education in a global perspective and a host of others. In addition, higher education should be made a separate, systematic discipline of graduate study at key, national-echelon universities, especially at the six teachers' universities under the direct administration of the State Education Commission.

Also to promote the development of a viable, dynamic system of higher education, it is recommended that systematic efforts be made in studying the higher education patterns and practices of other countries. In an attempt to modernize its higher education, the Chinese have been borrowing extensively from foreign experience ever since the late nineteenth century. But the efforts have been haphazard, resulting, at different times, in mechanical emulation without consideration of specific Chinese circumstances. In the 1950s, for example, there was the transplantation of the Soviet system, which led to serious consequences still perceivable today.

While it is essential to learn and absorb salient features of other systems, it should be remembered that a national education system is rooted in its cultural heritage and in the workings of an indigenous national life. Only by adopting a highly critical approach can the strengths of foreign systems be properly adapted and made to bear fruit on the Chinese soil. It is, therefore, recommended that the Chinese thoroughly acquaint themselves with different foreign systems, study their strengths and weaknesses and then introduce the applicable practices and patterns in the light of specific Chinese conditions instead of wholesale, indiscriminate borrowing in disregard of their own circumstances.

In addition to the commissioned research and the systematic study of foreign experience, it is recommended that universities and higher-education administrative authorities at various levels reinforce the institutes for higher-education research affiliated with over 200 colleges and universities. First, new personnel should be recruited for these institutes, which are largely made up of retired administrators. Second, adequate resources including library materials should be provided. Third, a national network should be established to facilitate coordination among these institutions.

Quality and Quantity

With the binary system of elite and mass sectors on the one hand and traditional and nontraditional institutions on the other, the quality-quantity issue which is inherent in Chinese higher education has become more prominent. The conflict or tension is vital for a viable higher education and, for that reason, may continue and perhaps be irreconcilable.

In any discussion of quality and quantity in Chinese higher eduction, one has to be constantly reminded that China is still a relatively poor and developing country which needs, first of all, a significant quantity of junior and secondary intellectual manpower. So it is recommended that the development of adult higher education, especially TV and correspondence courses, be given priority so that some form of postsecondary education can reach as many people as possible. With the widespread satellite receiving facilities, such courses can be made easily accessible to most parts of the nation, even to many of the remotest regions.

It is also recommended that community colleges be established, with at least one in every prefecture, which administers about ten counties. These colleges would draw financial support from local education taxes and from student tuition and fees. They would focus on agriculture and mechanical-arts courses geared to local needs. The students would consist of technicians sponsored by local industries and farms and rural high school graduates who make up about 70 percent of all high school graduates in the country. As only a very small percentage of these high school graduates are able to get into traditional colleges and universities, the local community colleges provide a welcome alternative not only for their future, but also for the benefit of the local rural economy.

A major practical difficulty for these suggested community colleges would be an adequate supply of competent faculty members. A concerted effort is needed to solve this problem. To begin with, all institutions of higher learning, not just the 300 teachers' colleges and universities, should undertake the training of teachers. As a matter of fact, many college graduates from non-teachers colleges and universities have been assigned teaching positions, particularly at the newly established colleges. With the gradual rise in pay and in social prestige, it is hoped that more college graduates will volunteer to take up teaching as a career.

Besides college graduates, these community colleges can absorb the surplus faculty from many well-established colleges and universities and invite, as adjunct professors, people from local industries, corporations and research institutes to lecture on special subjects. Local CCP and government leaders could be called upon to conduct related courses or seminars as well. Since these colleges would be locally oriented and community-sensitive, there is every reason for a close interaction between the colleges and the local administration and enterprises.

It is further recommended that graduates from these community colleges, from other types of non-traditional institutions of higher learning and from colleges offering short-cycle courses be allowed to compete for junior and senior years of studies at traditional four-year institutions through comprehensive examinations. By the same token, students enrolled in four-year colleges and universities should be screened after two years of undergraduate studies. Those who are not making satisfactory progress should be provided with job-oriented training and then be graduated with associate degrees. The competition would help to break the "Iron Rice Bowl" and invigorate or establish a new academic ethos.

The transfer function and the mid-selection would lead to quality teaching, which must be striven for at all levels and types of higher education. For this purpose, it is recommended that the SEC foster key institutions at all echelons and types of higher education, not just among long-standing, uniform traditional colleges and universities. In other words, centers of excellence or exemplary pacesetting institutions should be cultivated at every level and for every type of institution. Otherwise, the whole nation's higher education would emulate a few key colleges and universities, resulting in watered-down programs and a deterioration of standards.

The Aims of Higher Education

Along with continuous, drastic changes in China's political and economic spheres, the basic principles and aims of China's education have been prescribed and pursued in different ways. Before the late 1970s, undue emphasis was placed on the service of "proletarian" or CCP politics. Higher education became an extended arm for CCP rule and an appendage for party politics. Since the late 1970s when the nation shifted its emphasis from "proletarian revolution" to extensive economic development in an effort to modernize the country, education has been made to serve economic construction primarily.

Indeed, education in China has always served utilitarian functions. With their teaching and research facilities, colleges and universities have moved, over the years, to a prominent, central place. Along with this centrality have come many responsibilities, and in performing these responsibilities, higher education has become too practical in its purposes. As they pursue unfocused goals, colleges and universities have been offering a smorgasbord of courses to cater to the varying needs of a growing number of clients with little concern for quality and coherence.

If this trend is allowed to continue, Chinese colleges and universities may take, as their central purpose, the training of professionals instead of the education of generations of youth to be all-around men and women with fully developed potentials. It is, therefore, recommended that principles and aims of higher education be discussed and debated on a nationwide basis. Out of the discussion and debate, the true, fundamental aims and principles of higher education should be universally recognized and clearly prescribed. With the recognition, colleges and universities would be able to better adhere to their fundamental missions—the cultivation of men and women as fully developed human beings and the search for truth—while providing professional and technical training in specific fields of study and serving the society in a variety of ways.

To concentrate on the cultivation of men and women as well as the search for truth as the overriding concerns, it is recommended that colleges and universities use discretion and good judgment in accepting research projects and providing social services. They should not undertake tasks that can be discharged equally well by other organizations or lesser institutions established expressly for practical purposes. Only those programs that have the potential to enhance teaching and research and that command the interest and support of the faculty should be approved and undertaken.

Recommendations (Summarized)

The foregoing paragraphs discussed, in detail, the recommendations for the development of Chinese higher education during the decades ahead. These recommendations may be summarized as follows:

1) The State Education Commission, with the support and approval of the National People's Congress, should draft and enact laws concerning higher education so that it will be less vulnerable to political expediencies.

2) An index of educational appropriations relative to the nation's economic growth should be stipulated by law and alternative sources of funding be encouraged and regulated. While striving for an increase in funding, it is imperative to improve management. These improvements include increasing the low teacher-student ratio to 1:10,

enlarging the university size to an average of 3000 to 5000 students, and contracting support services to other social organizations.

3) Systematic, thorough research on higher education should be conducted to ensure that higher education develop on a rational basis. In order to produce desirable, relevant research, it is recommended that higher education be made a discipline of graduate study at leading Chinese universities.

4) The number of community colleges with vocational, technical programs should be increased to meet the pressing need of China's socioeconomic development. In the meantime, mechanisms for competition be introduced to ensure the quality of higher education.

5) Fundamental aims of higher education for China should be arrived at through free, democratic debate. While training technical and professional manpower and providing social services, colleges and universities adhere to their central missions—the cultivation of men and women and the search for truth.

Postscript

Higher education is seldom a static institution, but its reform is a protracted, complex process. The decade of 1978-1988 witnessed extensive reforms and notable achievements as well as the problems that had emerged or been exacerbated in the reform process. As China is a developing country with much untapped potential, its higher education—an integral part of the nation's political and economic structure—has great potential for future reform and development.

To maintain the dynamism of the reform that began in the late 1970s and establish, in the current Chinese parlance, a higher-education system with Chinese characteristics, Chinese higher education must look backward, outward and forward, fusing its own rich heritage and experience with appropriate foreign practices and patterns to meet the challenges of the twenty-first century. But under a relatively centralized system of government, reform in higher education is invariably conditioned by the pace and direction of the nation's political and economic development. Since China is advancing with occasional, temporary setbacks, its higher education will encounter new, continual problems. However, as history never turns back, China's higher education will move forward with its due service to the Chinese nation and contribution to the whole of mankind.

REFERENCES

Asiaweek. February 2, 1990, p. 6.

Bai, Jingyu. (1989). Personal correspondence. August 3 and November 26.

Bai, Nanfeng. (1987). Young people's attitudes and aspirations: Will they welcome reform? In Bruce L. Reynolds, ed., *Reform in China: Challenges & Choices.* Armonk, New York: M. E. Sharpe, Inc., pp. 161-182.

Ban, Rongxue. (1989). Personal correspondence. November 15.

Barrow, John. (1948). American institutions of higher learning in China. *Higher Education. 4* (11), 121-124.

Bastid, Marianne. (1987). Servitude or liberation? The introduction of foreign educational practices and systems to China since 1940. In Ruth Hayhoe & Marianne Bastid, eds., *China's Education and the Industrialized World.* Armonk, New York: M. E. Sharpe, Inc., pp. 3-20.

Best, John W., & Kahn, James V. (1989). *Research in Education.* Englewood Cliffs, New Jersey: Prentice Hall.

Bok, Derek. (1982). *Beyond the Ivory Tower: Social Responsibilities of the Modern University.* Cambridge, Massachusetts: Harvard University Press.

Briant, Jacobs. (1989). Personal interview. August 15.

Brubacher, John S., & Rudy, Willis. (1976). *Higher Education in Transition* (Third edition revised and enlarged). New York: Harper & Row.

Burn, Barbara B. (1980). *Expanding the International Dimension of Higher Education.* San Francisco: Jossey-Bass Publishers

Cai, Keyong & Zhao, Wei. (1987). Dui woguo gaojiao cunci jiegude tansuo [Explorations of our country's higher education structure by level]. In Hao Keming & Wang Yongquan, eds., *Zhongguo Gaodeng Jiaoyu Jiegou Yanjiu [Studies of the Structure of Chinese Higher Education].* Beijing: People's Education Press, pp. 39-65

Cai, Keyong. (1982). *Gaideng Jiaoyu Jianshi [A Short History of Higher Education].* Wuhan, China: Huazhong College of Science and Technology Press

CCP Central committee. (1961). *Provisional Stipulations Governing Institutions of Higher Learning under the Ministry of Education (Sixty Articles)*

CCP Central Committee. (1978). *Communique of the Third Plenary Session of the 11th Central Committee of the Chinese Communist Party*

CCP Central Committee. (1984). *Decision of the Central Committee of the CCP on the Reform of the Economic Structure*

CCP Central Committee. (1985). *Decision of the Central Committee of the Chinese Communist Party on the Reform of the Educational System*

CCP Central Committee & State Council. (1958). *Directives Concerning Education*

Central Institute for Educational Research (CIER). (1983). *Zhongguo Jiaoyu Dashiji: 1949-1982 [A Chronicle of Chinese Education: 1949-1982]*. Beijing: Educational Science Press

Chang, David. (1989). Personal interview, May, 7

Chen, Yi. (1962). *Speech at a Guangzhou Meeting*. March 5, 1962

Chen, Zhenyi. (1985). Waiyu jiaoyu yingdang gaike [Foreign language teaching should be reformed]. *Renmin Ribao [People's Daily]*. June 23, 1985, p. 5

Cheng, Yuan. (1989). Daxueshengde sixiang wuquyu shehuide wudao [Mistakes of college students and social misguidance]. *Renmin Ribao [People's Daily]*. September 11 & 12, p. 2

China Daily. April 4, 1990, p. 3; April 6, 1989, p. 4; December 25, 1986, p. 4; November 30, 1984, p. 4

China Education Yearbook: 1949-1984 [Local Education]. (1986) Changsha, China: Hunan Education Press

China Exchange News (CEN). *17* (1), 24, 1989; *13* (2), 38-39, 40, 1985; *13* (3), 16-24, 1985; *13* (1), 31

China Handbook Editorial Committee (CHEC). (1983). *Education and Science*. Beijing: Foreign Languages Publishing House

China Statistical Bureau. (1989). Education in present-day China *Beijing Review*. July 17-23, pp. 25-27

Chronicle of Higher Education. November, 22, 1989, p. A25

Circular on Military Training at Selected Schools. (1985). Xinhua Domestic Service, Beijing. In *China Report*, No. 19, March 1, 1985, pp. 49-49

Cleverley, John. (1985). *The School of China: Tradition and Modernity in Chinese Education*. Sydney: G. Allen & Unwin

Clough, Ralph N. (1981). *A Review of the U.S.-China Exchange Program*. Washington D.C.: Office of Research, International Agency, United States of America

Confucius & Mencius. (1966). *The Four Books* (James Legge, trans.). Taipei: Dadong Book Company

Craig, Marshall. (1989). Personal interview, June 23

Croizier, Ralph C. (1979). Education and culture. In Harold C. Hinton, ed., *The People's Republic of China: A Handbook*. Boulder, Colorado: Westview Press

Deng, Xiaoping. (1983). Autograph to the Beijing Jingshan School

Deng, Xiaoping. (1984). *Selected Works of Deng Xiaoping (1975-1982)*. Beijing: Foreign Languages Publishing House, pp. 101-126

Du, Gui. (1990). Xuezi chengcai yingtong cuguo fazhan jinmi jiehe [Academic endeavors should be closely linked with the country's development]. *Zhongguo Qingnian Bao [China Youth Daily]*. March 20, 1990, p. 2

Fairbank, John, & Reischauer, Edwin O. (1978). *China: Transition and Transformation*. Boston: Houghton Mifflin Company

Falkenheim, Victor C., ed. (1989). *Chinese Politics from Mao to Deng.* New York: Paragon House

Fingar, Thomas, & Reed, Linda A. (1982). *An Introduction to Education in the People's Republic of China and U.S.- China Educational Exchanges.* Washington D.C.: Committee on Scholarly Communication with the PRC (CSCPRC) & National Association for Foreign Students Affairs.

Fisher, James L. (1984). *Power of the Presidency.* New York: Macmillan

Fu, Xingguo, & Yang, Xiumei. (1989). Woguo jiaoyu tizhi gaige chengjiu he jinyibu shenhua de sikao [Achievements of the reform of our country's education system and thoughts on its further development]. *Journal of Beijing Normal University. 3,* 92-97

Gao, Shangqin. (1988). Putong gaoxiao zhaoshou zifeisheng [Traditional institutions of higher learning enrolling self- financed students]. *Zhongguo Gaodeng Jiaoyu [Chinese Higher Education]. 6,* 23-23

Gardner, John. (1982). *Chinese Politics and the Succession to Mao.* London: Macmillan

Gay, L. R. (1987). *Educational Research: Competencies for Analysis and Application* (3rd edition). Columbus: Charles E. Merrill Publishing Company

Gong, Yingbin. (1988). Tigao yanjiusheng shuzhide yixiang gaige cuoshi [A measure to raise the quality of graduate students]. *Zhongguo Gaodeng Jiaoyu [Chinese Higher Education]. 2,* 39-41

Gu, Mingyuan. (1984). The development and reform of higher education. *Comparative Education. 20* (1), 141-149

Guan, Yinong. (1988). Guanyu zhubu wanshan daxuesheng junxun zhidude jidian jianyi [Suggestions on gradually improving the military training for college students]. *Zhongguo Gaodeng Jiaoyu [Chinese Higher Education]. 7-8,* 66-67

Guangming Ribao [Guangming Daily]. October 9, p. 3; October 9, 1989, p. 1; September 22, 1989, p. 2; August 1, 1988, p. 2; January 30, 1988, p. 3; December 4, 1988 p. 2; October 24, 1987, p. 1; October 24, 1987, p. 3; March 15, 1987, p. 3;

Hamrin, Carol L. (1987). Conclusion: New trends under Deng Xiaoping and his successors. In Merle Goldman with Timothy Cheek and Carol Lee Hamrin, eds. *China's Intellectuals and the State: In Search of a New Relationship.* Cambridge, Massachusetts: Council on East Asian Studies, Harvard University, pp. 275-304

Han, Daniel. (1989). Personal interview, August 31

Han, Wencai, & Wu, Rongqing. (1989). Guanyu jiaoyu chaoqian fazhan [On education taking precedence in development]. *Liaowang Zhoukan [Liaowang Weekly,* Overseas Edition]. June 26, pp. 52-53

Hao, Keming, & Wang, Yongquan, eds. (1987). *Zhongguo Gaodeng Jiaoyu Jiegou Yanjiu [Studies of the Structure of Chinese Higher Education].* Beijing: People's Education Press

Hawkins, John N. (1984). Educational exchanges and the transformation of higher education in the PRC. In Elinor G. Barber, Philip G. Altbach, & Robert G. Myers, eds., *Bridges to Knowledge: Foreign Students in Comparative Perspective.* Chicago: University of Chicago Press, pp. 19-31

Hayhoe, Ruth. (1984). The evolution of modern Chinese educational institutions. In Ruth Hayhoe (Ed.), *Contemporary Chinese Education.* London: Croom Helm, pp. 26-46

Hayhoe, Ruth. (1989). *Chinese Universities and the Open Door.* Armonk, New York: M. E. Sharpe, Inc

He, Bozhuan. (1986). Zhongguo jiaoyude shida weiji [The ten crises in Chinese education]. *Zhongguo Renmin Daxue Fuying Ziliao [The Chinese People's University Reprint Series]* Beijing: People's University Press. pp. 25-27

He, Dongchang. (1989). Education: opening and improvement. *Beijing Review.* September 25 - October 1, pp. 35-36

Henze, Juergen. (1984). Higher education: The tension between quality and equality. In Ruth Hayhoe, ed., *Contemporary Chinese Education.* Armonk, New York: M.E. Sharpe, Inc., pp. 93-153

Hou, Ruili. (1990). Population problems on the eve of the 1990 census. *China Today.* Vol. XXXIX, No. 31, pp. 26-29.

Hu, Shiming, & Seifman, Eli, eds. (1987). *Education and Socialist Modernization: A Documentary History of Education in the PRC, 1977-1986.* New York: Ams Press

Hu, Yaobang. (1982). Create a new situation in all fields of socialist modernization. (Report to the 12th National Congress of the CCP, September 1, 1982). *Beijing Review. 25* (37), 11-46

Hu, Zhuanglin. (1989). Personal correspondence. October, 13

Hua, Yi. (1988). Zouchu erlu beifande lishi shengu (1): Jiaoyu gaigeyu gaigezhongde chongtu [Abyss of the antinomies (1): Conflicts and new choices in China's educational reform] *Gaojiao Yanjiuyu Tansuo (Research on Higher Education). 3,* 9-17

Huang, Shiqi. (1985, October). The training and professional development of academic staff in the PRC. Paper presented at the International Workshop on Professional Development of Academic Staff and Its Management, Shanghai, China.

Huang Shiqi. (1987). Contemporary educational relations with the industrialized world: A Chinese view. In Ruth Hayhoe, & Marianne Bastid, eds. *China's Education and the Industrialized World.* Armonk, New York: M. E. Sharpe, Inc pp. 225-251

Huang, Xinbai. (1988). Press Release, Embassy of the PRC in Washington D.C., April 8

Ji, Jingxia. (1989). Amateur college attracts attention. *Beijing Review.* July 17-23: 34-35

Jiang, Zemin. (1990). Xiwan huanchai nimen shenshang [Our hopes are still placed on you]. *Shenzhou Xueren [China's Scholars Abroad].* 18, 2: 1

Johnson, Todd M. (1989). The economics of higher education reform in China. *China Exchange News (CEN)*. *17* (1), 3-7.

Kanter, Stephen. (1985). Socratic sipping: Teaching law in China. *China Exchange News (CEN)*. *13* (3), 7-12

Lavroff, D. G. (1985). The international roots of higher education. In William H. Allaway, & Hallam C. Shorrock, eds. *Dimensions of International Higher Education*. Boulder: Westview Press, pp. 13-18.

Li, Bin. (1989). Study Blahs hit students. *Beijing Review*. *32* (6), 11-12

Li, Keming. (1985). Huanan shifan daxue gaigede chubu shijian [Initial reform in South China Teachers University]. *Zhongguo Renmin Daxue Fuying Ziliao [The Chinese People's University Reprint Series]*. Beijing: People's University Press, pp. 19-24

Li, Li. (1988). Higher education: Reforming and restructuring the system. *Beijing Review*. *31* (24), 25-30

Li, Lin. (1988). Qiantan gaoxiao shizi buchong [Preliminary thoughts on replenishing the academic staff of institutions of higher learning]. *Zhongguo Gaodeng Jiaoyu [Chinese Higher Education]*. *11*, 39-40

Li, Peng. (1986). Guanyu gaodeng jiaoyu gaige yu fazhan de ruogan wenti [Problems on the reform and development of higher education]. *Zhongguo Gaodeng Jiaoyu [Chinese Higher Education]*. *7*, 1-5

Li, Tieying. (1988). Li Tieying tan liuxuesheng zhence [Li Tieying on policies governing students studying overseas]*Shenzhou Xueren [China's Scholars Abroad]*. *6, 9*

Li, Tieying. (1989). Interview by reporters. *Renmin Ribao [People's Daily, Overseas Edition]*. March 25, p. 3

Li, Youzhi. (1989). Huanqi quanminzu dui jiaoyu weijide gongshi [Arouse the awareness of the whole nation to the education crisis]. *Zhongguo Qingnian Bao [China Youth Daily]*. March 6, p. 3

Liang, Younen. (1988). Shenhua jiaoyu gaigede jidian shexiang [Thought on deepening educational reform]. *Zhongguo Gaodeng Jiaoyu [Chinese Higher Education]*. *12, 39-40*

Lin, Chongde. (1989). Personal correspondence, September 14, 1989.

Liu, Luxia. (1985). Qinghua Daxuetongguo duo qudaocujin keji yujingji jiehe [Qinghua University promotes integration of science, technology and economy through diverse channels]. *Guangming Ribao [Guangming Daily]*. March 13, p. 1

Liu, Zhangxi. (1989). Jiaoyu yeyao zhongshi neibu waqian [It is also imperative for education to tap its own potential]. *Renmin Ribao [People's Daily, Overseas Edition]* November 17, pp. 5-7

Liu, Zhongde. (1987). Guanyu gaojiao shiye fazhanzhong de jige wenti [Questions concerning the development of higher education]. *Zhongguo Gaodeng Jiaoyu [Chinese Higher Education]*. *5*, 2-4

Liu, Zhongde. (1988). Guanyu qiwuhou sannian gaojiao fazhanji anpai jinnian zhaosheng jihua gongzhuode jidian yijian [On the development of higher education during the last three years of the Seventh Five-Year Plan and this year's enrollment plan]. *Zhongguo Gaodeng Jiaoyu [Chinese Higher Education]. 5*, 7-13

Long, Zhengzhong. (1989). Shenhua gaodeng zhuanke jiaoyu gaigede jige wenti [Questions on deepening short-cycle higher education]. *Zhongguo Gaodeng Jiaoyu [Chinese Higher Education]. 1*, 10-13

Lu, Shihai. (1989). Zhishi fengzi daiyu piandi wentide xiangzhuang pinggu, gengyuan paoxiyu duice xuanze [Evaluations of the low remuneration to intellectuals, analysis of the cause, and the selection of measures]. *Jingji Kexue [Economic Science]. 50*, 6-10

Lu, Yongxiang. (1989). Zhejiang daxue shishi zonghe gaigede chubu zhuofahe shexiang. [Preliminary steps and plans for a comprehensive reform at Zhejiang University]. *Zhongguo Gaodeng Jiaoyu [Chinese Higher Education]. 2*, 2-4

Maddox, Patrick G., & Thurston, Anne F. (1987). Academic exchanges: The goals and roles of U.S. universities. In Joyce K. Kallgren & Denis Fred Simon, eds. *Educational Exchanges: Essays on the Sino-American Experience* . University of California, Berkeley: Institute of East Asian Studies, pp. 119-148.

Mao, Zedong. (1977). On the correct handling of contradictions among the people. *Selected Works of Mao Zedong*. Volume 5, pp. 384-421

Ministry of Education (MOE). (1985). *Achievement of Education in China 1949-1983*. Beijing: People's Education Press.

Nanjing-Johns Hopkins Center. (1989). *An Introduction to Nanjing-Johns Hopkins Center*

Northeast College of Technology (Dongbei Gongxueyuan jiaoshi gongzuochu). (1988). Duocunci kaizhan shizi peixun gongzuo [Undertake teacher training at multilevels]. *Zhongguo Gaodeng Jiaoyu [Chinese Higher Education]. 8*, 26-27

Oksenburg, Michael. (1989). Foreword. In John Woodruff, *China: In Search of Its Future*. Seattle: University of Washington Press.

Orleans, Leo A. (1988). *Chinese Students in America: Policies, Issues, and Numbers*. Washington D.C.: National Academy Press

Orleans, Leo A. (1989a). China's changing attitude toward the brain drain and policy toward returned students. *China Exchange News (CEN). 17* (2), 2-5

Orleans, Leo A. (1989b). Chinese in America: The numbers game. *China Exchange News (CEN). 17* (3), 9-10

Pan, Junqi. (1987). Kaizhan henxiang lianxi, wei jinji jianshe fuwu, cujingaoxiao jiaoyu shenru fazhan [Establish horizontal links, serve the economic development, and deepen educational reform at colleges and universities]. *Zhongguo Gaodeng Jiaoyu [Chinese Higher Education]. 10*, 27-28

Pepper, Suzanne. (1982). China universities: New experiments in socialist democracy and administrative reform. *Modern China. 8* (2), 147-204

References **139**

President's Office, Zhejiang University. (1988). *Zhejiang Daxuezonghe Gaige Fangan [Plans for the Comprehensive Reform at Zhejiang University]*. Hangzhou, Zhejiang University
Pretzer, Wallace. (1989). Personal interview, September 2
Qiao, Hong. (1989). Gaoxiao qingnian xuesheng redian chengyin jiqi daoxiang [Reason and guidance of the hot spots of young students at colleges and universities]. *Zhongguo Qingnian Bao [China Youth Daily]*. November 11, p. 3
Qu, Qinyue. (1988, July). Fazhan, Gaige, Kaifang, Sikao [Development, reform, opening, and reflection]. Address at the 3rd Sino-U.S. University President Conference, Nanjing, China
Reed, Linda A. (1988). *Education in the PRC and U.S.-China Educational Exchanges*. Washington D.C.: National Association for Foreign Student Affairs
Ren, Zhong. (1987). Jilinshen gaodeng jiaoyu kelei jiegude yanjiu [Studies of the curricular structure of higher education in Jilin Province]. In Hao Keming, & Wang Yongquan (Eds.). *Zhongguo Gaodeng Jiaoyu Jiegou Yanjiu [Studies of the Structure of Chinese Higher Education]* Beijing: People's Education Press, pp. 178-184
Renmin Ribao [People's Daily, Overseas Edition]. April 13, 1990, p. 1; May 7, 1990, p. 1
Richardson, Timothy. (1989). Personal interview, July 13
Rosemont, Henry, Jr. (1985). Fudan University: Showcasing China's new educational policies. *Change. 17* (2), 41-45
Rosen, Stanley. (1985). Decentralization, recentralization, and rationalization. *Modern China*. July 1985, pp. 301-436.
Rubin, Kyna. (1983). Higher education in China: Recent calls for reform. *China Exchange News (CEN). 11* (2), 34-36
Shen, Youtai. (1989). Personal correspondence. March 4
Shen, Youtai. (1990). Personal correspondence. July 5
Shive, Glenn. (1990). Policy debates and rumor mills: China's emerging restrictions on study abroad. In Carol Strevy, *Financial Status of Students/Scholars from the PRC on U.S.Campuses*. New York: Institute of International Education (IIE)
Shu, Zijia. (1988). Baguonei fangwen xuezhede jieshouyu xuanpai gongzhuo tuijin yibu [Promote the work of visiting scholars at Chinese universities]. *Zhongguo Gaodeng Jiaoyu [Chinese Higher Education]. 8*, 29-31
State Education Commission. (1986). *Achievement of Education in China: Statistics (1980-1985)*. Beijing: People's Education Press
State Education Commission. (1987). *Certain Interim Provisions of the State Education Commission on the Work of Sending Personnel to Study Abroad*. Beijing: SEC
State Education Commission. (1988). *A Survey of Education in China*. Beijing: SEC

State Education Commission. (1989). *Education in China (1978-1988)*. Beijing: SEC

Stavis, Benedict. (1988). *China's Political Reform: An Interim Report*. New York: Praeger

Strevy, Carol. (1990). *Financial Status of Students/Scholars from the PRC on U.S. Campuses*. New York: Institute of International Education (IIE)

Sun, Tianyi. (1989). Personal correspondence. September 23 and November 16

Tao, Yazhen. (1989). Personal correspondence. September 30 and November 18

Third Department, SEC. (1988). *Post-Secondary Education in China: Present State and Trends*. Beijing: SEC

United Nations Education, Science, and Culture Organization (UNESCO). (1988). *Statistical Yearbook 1988*. Paris: UNESCO

Wang, Baiyu. (1989). Personal correspondence. August 16

Wang, Jiping. (1988). Bixu jiaqiang duogaodeng jiaoyu zixue kaoshide jihuahe guanli [It is imperative to strengthen planning and management of the college exams for the self-taught students]. *Zhongguo Gaodeng Jiaoyu [Chinese Higher Education]. 12*, 34-37

Wang, Naidong. (1990). Personal interview. February 15

Wang Shih-chieh. (1936). Education. In Chao-Ying Shih & Chi-Hsien Chang, eds. *The Chinese Yearbook (1936-37)*. Shanghai: The Commercial Press, Limited, pp. 450-523

Wang, Yibing. (1985). Updating China's education system. *Beijing Review. 28* (50), 15-17

Wang, Yibing. (1985). Tasks set for educational reform. *Beijing Review. 28* (51), 19-22

Wang, Yibing. (1985). China's education holds bright prospects.*Beijing Review. 28* (52), 21-23

Wang, Yongquan. (1987, November). The structure and governance of Chinese higher education. Paper presented at the 4th International Seminar on Higher Education in Asia, Hiroshima City, Japan

Wang, Zheng. (1988). College programs for young science prodigies. *China Reconstructs. 35* (3), 42-45

Wei, Liming. (1989). Better conditions for returned students. *Beijing Review*. March 13-19, pp. 23-28

Wei, Wei. (1989). Overseas students: The world of education. *Beijing Review*. March 13-19, pp.19-23

Wei, Zhi. (1984). Jiji gaige zhaosheng laiyuan jihua [Actively reform the enrollment source plan] *Gaojiao Zhanxian [Higher Education Front]. 5*, 22-24

World Bank. (1983). *China: Socialist Economic Development: The Social Sector, Population, Health, Nutrition and Education*. The World Bank: Washington, D.C

World Bank. (1985a). *China: Long-Term Development Issues and Options*. Baltimore: Johns Hopkins University Press

World Bank. (1985b). *China: Issues and Prospects In Education.* The World Bank: Washington, D.C

World Bank. (1986). *China: Management and Finance of Higher Education.* The World Bank: Washington, D.C

Wu, Genliang. (1988). Lun zhongguo jindai liuxuesheng de lishi zuoyong [On the historical role of returned students in modern history]. *Wenhui Bao [Wenhui Daily].* March 25, p. 4

Wu, Xingke. (1989). Dangdai daxueshengde xintai tedianji jiazhi quxiang [Psychological characteristics and trends in value judgment among contemporary college students]. *Zhongguo Qingnian Bao [China Youth Daily].* November 13, p. 3

Wu, Zhuoqun. (1988, July). Woguo daxue xiaozhangde zhuoyong he mianlingde wenti [University presidents in our country: their roles and problems]. Paper presented at the 3rd Sino-U.S. University President Conference, Nanjing, China.

Xiao, Guangen. (1988). Gei xuexiao chuangshu kailudeng [Turn green light to the money-making endeavor of universities] *Renmin Ribao [People's Daily,* Overseas edition], October 10, 1988, p. 3

Xiao, Hang. (1986). Buneng hushi chuguo re [We mustn't ignore the study-abroad fever]. *Gaojiao Zhanxian [Higher Education Front]. 3,* 4-6

Xiao, Yuankai. (1989). TV university: Alternate road to learning. *China Reconstructs. XXXVIII* (6), 28-30

Xinguancha. [News Observe]. (1989). University students do business. *Beijing Review.* May 8-14, p. 41

Xu, Donghunag. (1989). Tan yange kunzhi gaodeng xuexiao fazhan guimo wenti [On the strict control of the increase of colleges and universities]. *Zhongguo Gaodeng Jiaoyu [Chinese Higher Education]. 2,* 5-7.

Yang, Deguang. (1989). Personal correspondence. November 24

Yang, Xiaobing. (1988). CPPCC members on state affairs. *Beijing Review.* April 18-24, pp. 21-23

Yang, Xingguan. (1986). Duiwan kaifangzhong de wenhua yingjin yu jiaoliu [Cultural imports and exchanges in the course of opening up to the outside world]. *Guangming Ribao [Guangming Daily].* June 7, 1986, p. 3

Yang, Xun. (1990). Personal correspondence. December 24

Yao, Yi. (1985). Shiying kexuejishu fazhande qushi, Beida wei wenkexuesheng kaishe jinsibaimen xuanxiuke [To adapt to the trend in scientific and technological development, Beijing University offers nearly four hundred electives for humanities students]. *Zhongguo Jiaoyu Bao [China Education News].* March 2, p. 1.

Ye, Chunsheng. (1987). Duozhong xinshi lianhe banxue, cujin gaodeng jiaoyu wenbu fazhan, tigao zhiliang [Collaborate in running schools through diverse means, promote stable development of higher education and raise quality]. *Zhongguo Gaodeng Jiaoyu [Chinese Higher Education]. 6,* 23-24

Yi, Nong. (1988). Lunlianhe juban chengren gaodeng jiaoyu [On combined efforts in running adult higher education]. *Zhongguo Gaodeng Jiaoyu [Chinese Higher Education]. 6,* 40- 41

Yu, Fusheng. (1989). Interview with *Ban Yue Tan [Fortnightly Chat].* No. 2, January 23, p. 11

Yuan, Yunkai. (1988). Jiaqiang dui yiuxiu qingnian jiaoshide fuzhi peiyang [Help and train outstanding young teachers]. *Zhongguo Gaodeng Jiaoyu [Chinese Higher Education]. 9,* 27- 29

Zhang, Qizi. (1989). Personal correspondence. December 27

Zhang, Shihuang & Zhu, Jizhou. (1987). Gaohuo rencai peiyang guochengde tansuo [Studies on invigorating the training of personnel]. *Zhongguo Gaodeng Jiaoyu [Chinese Higher Education]. 2,* 25-26

Zhang, Shuren. (1988). Dui gaodeng xuexiao henxiang lianhede jidian renshi [Thoughts on the horizontal links among institutions of higher learning]. *Zhongguo Gaodeng Jiaoyu [Chinese Higher Education]. 4,* 15-18

Zhang, Xiaowen. (1988, July). Zhongguo gaodeng jiaoyude duiwai kaifang [The Opening of Chinese Higher Education]. Paper presented at the 3rd Sino-U.S. University President Conference, Nanjing, China.

Zhao, Juncheng. (1989). Personal correspondence. December 5

Zhao, Wei. (1989). Xuehui guanzhu weilai [Learn to pay close attention to the future]. *Liaowang Zhoukan [Liaowang Weekly,* Overseas edition], pp. 30-31

Zhao, Ziyang. (1987). Advance along the road of socialism with Chinese characteristics. (Report to the 13th National Congress of the CCP, December 25, 1987). *Beijing Review. 30* (45), 23-49

Zhen, Heling. (1989). Shantou daxuehe Li Jiacheng [Shantou University and Li Jiacheng]. *Renmin Ribao [People's Daily,* Overseas edition]. September 26, p. 4

Zhong, Guangxue. (1989). Personal interviews. November 12 and November 23

Zhongguo Jiaoyu Bao [China Education News]. July 8, 1986, p. 1

Zhongguo Qingnian Bao [China Youth Daily]. April 13, 1989, p. 1 January 30, 1989, p. 3

Zhou, L. X. (1989). Personal interview. December 8

Zhu, Fengsheng. (1990). Personal correspondence. April 15

Zhu, Kaixuan. (1988). Guanche shisanda jingshen, shenhuahe jiakuai gaodeng jiaoyude gaige [Carry out the spirit of the 13th CCP national congress, deepen and quicken higher education reform]. *Zhongguo Gaodeng Jiaoyu [Chinese Higher Education]. 4,* 5-14.

INDEX

Academic apathy, 86, 92
Academic committees, 64
Academic degrees, 81-2, 91
  bachelor's, 81, 82
  MA, 81, 82
  Ph.D., 82
  regulations governing, 81, 82
Academic promotion, 74
Adult education, 12, 35-40, 42
  TV university, 35-7, 127
  staff/worker university, 37
  farmer university, 37
  management personnel
    university, 37
  correspondence courses, 12, 38-9
  night school, 38-9
  educational colleges, 38
  examinations for self-taught, 39
Aims, 128-9, 130
Anti-Rightist Campaign, 10, 72
Australia, 98, 99
Beijing Agricultural University, 51
Beijing Foreign StudiesUniversity,
  54
Beijing Normal University, 24, 70
Beijing University, 24, 25, 29, 32,
  50, 81, 86
Borrowing of foreign models, 4-5
Boxer Indemnity, 93
Brain drain
  extent of, 101, 110
  reasons of, 101-2
  attitude toward, 102, 104, 110
  U.S. and China's brain drain,
    104-6
  rationale of, 103-4
Brubacher, John S, 56
Buddhism, 2
Canada, 94

Carnegie Foundation, 125
Categories of colleges and universities, 29-30
CCP (Chinese Communist Party),
  1, 5, 6, 7, 10, 11, 15, 16, 17, 26,
  28, 33, 40, 41, 62, 72, 76, 79,
  83, 87, 88, 89, 90, 91, 95, 97,
  101, 108, 120, 121, 128
CCPUP (Chinese Communist Party
  university committee), 11, 26,
  27, 40, 41
CEAIE (Chinese Education Associ-
  ation for International Ex-
  change), 99
Central Land Reclamation Bureau,
  53
Central TV University, 35
Centralization in the 1950s, 7-8
Chinese Academy of Sciences, 80
Chinese Academy of Social Sci-
  ences, 80
Chinese People's Political Consul-
  tative Committee, 40
Chinese People's University, 44
Chinese Returned Students Service
  Center, 107
Chinese University of Science &
  Technology, 78
Clough, Ralph N, 105
College entrance examinations, 75,
  76-7, 91 see also enrollment
Colleges in Communist areas, 5-6
Community colleges, 34, 41-2,
  118, 128, 130
Confucius, 1, 2, 3, 4, 8, 16, 73, 103
  doctrine of, 1
  Confucian higher education, 2-3
  philosophy of, 2
Correspondence courses, 12, 127